CHANGE LEADERSHIP

Making a Positive Difference as a Visible and Deliberate Creator of Rapid Change

JO SINGEL

Lulu Publishing Services rev. date: 06/19/2019

INTRODUCTION

WHY READ THIS BOOK?

BY THE END OF READING AND DOING THE WORK...

...you will have created a **vision** for your own personal leadership. You have identified **obstacles** to achieving your desires. You have examined **assumptions, beliefs and attitudes** that might derail your progress. You've cleared out the **baggage** of past experiences and your history to make room for the future. You will take these **goals**, attitudes and desires into the world and create your own **inspiring messages of leadership.**

What you will know: Being in leadership will place you in situations where your thinking will be put to the test. High levels of self-awareness are key. It is essential your messages are consistent, elegant, clear and congruent. Being in integrity and being authentic will differentiate you. Your self-generated Life Story Timeline is your guide for safely navigating the complexities of change.

What you will understand: Visions are rarely fulfilled as the complete result of our own actions and activities. You have strategies for aligning, influencing, persuading, or selling your ideas and enrolling the commitment of others to a common consciousness.

What you will gain in wisdom...Leadership is always involved in change of any kind. As a leader, you have a deeper knowledge of what it takes to accelerate the rate of change creation through an enlightened, motivating and energizing change process that works; an appreciation and empathy for how and why people change or resist the new approach. You have the necessary tools and extra steps needed for reducing the risk of failure while enhancing the opportunity for success. You are applying what you've learned and are sharing your knowledge to help others learn, grow and evolve.

YOU NOW HAVE THE TOOLS FOR "MAKING A POSITIVE DIFFERENCE AS A VISIBLE AND DELIBERATE CREATOR OF RAPID CHANGE".

ARE YOU READY FOR THE JOURNEY?

The following questions require only a "yes or no" answer:

1. Am I sufficiently dissatisfied with the way things are now that I am willing to invest the time and energy in being a "visible and deliberate creator of rapid change"?
2. Will I be able to build up enough momentum so that I get past the wall of inertia, fear and intimidation I'll feel when I reach the point where I am paralyzed by the magnitude of what I am attempting to do?
3. Do I have the guts to take those first steps?
4. And if I can't, do I have the courage to ask for help?

If you have responded "yes", this book will ground you in creating a life and destiny you desire. Taking up leadership encompasses every aspect of your life. Going a step further is what this book is about. Choosing to be a leader is the first step. Choosing to "Make a positive difference as a visible and deliberate creator of rapid change" is the next and most powerful step.

Let's get going.

HOW TO USE THIS BOOK

The book is organized around key concepts of learning and leadership development. In this book, we learn through experience, by learning a concept, designing an action, applying the action, reflecting on what worked and didn't work, and then applying the new learning into a continuous feedback loop.

You will learn theories regarding change, leadership, learning and effective organizational tasks such as team development, group dynamics and collaboration. Creating Learning Partnerships, Mentoring, and building a Life Story Timeline enlighten, broaden, stretch and enhance the unfoldment of one's vision for a lifetime and legacy of meaningful growth and evolvement.

A special consideration and understanding needs to be made regarding the subject of CONFLICT. It is the philosophy of the Author that conflict is a given part of life and most especially in being in leadership whether as a stand one takes or a role of authority. All the approaches, activities and ideas suggested in the material presented in this book represent a professional lifetime of studying and teaching conflict management and resolution. Conflict is assumed when any change is indicated, initiated and implemented. Conflict is inherent in the process and therefore is not treated separately but rather integrated into the development of leadership and the implementation of any change initiative whether for self, others or organizations.

Throughout the book there are RULES for the journey, strategies, stories, frameworks and other tools. The book is iterative as it is set up as a process and series of activities interspersed with questions, reflection moments and some repetition as the material goes deeper into the topic of being in leadership in life.

Learning, growing and evolving as a self-development commitment is emphasized. There are materials for those either in current roles of leadership or aspiring to be a leader of others. Tip sheets, check lists and other guidelines and strategies are provided and are meant to be overviews and sources of inspiration and taking action quickly and effectively. Given that learning anything is a process, all leaders are encouraged to dig deeper into all topics and build additional resources around them.

As a value-add, by the end of doing the work in this book, not only will you have the map for your continued leadership development as a leader in life, work and community, you will also be able to initiate and effectively implement a social impact initiative and or a corporate social responsibility goal.

The desire and goal of the book is to act as a solid foundation, an inspiration, a guide along the journey only you can walk and build upon as you proceed with your own desires and aspirations for your life.

A lifetime of passionate interest, the influence of leaders, mentors and teachers are infused into every word and passage. Imagine all of those voices and their experiences urging you on to fulfill a destiny you desire and that you have the potential to create for yourself, others and the world. That is the promise and fulfillment of leadership.

Lead your life on purpose.

Take ownership.

It will make the difference

between abundance or scarcity.

- Jo Singel

TURBULENCE AHEAD

Imagine you are seated in an airplane that has cruised smoothly down the runway. The plane safely achieves lift off and you are gradually and steadily climbing 10,000, 20,000 and ultimately 30,000 feet to achieve your cruising height.

You are finally relaxing and are looking forward to removing your seat belt and standing in the narrow aisle to stretch your legs that have been imprisoned by the cramped space you have been occupying during the flight.

No sooner than you complete the thought, the overhead light blinks and you can hear the gravelly sound of the airplane's intercom system. The pilot clears her throat as she prepares to make an announcement. You expect good news; with a good tailwind, you might arrive at your destination ahead of schedule. Instead, the pilot describes a less desirable scenario. There will be unexpected and severe turbulence caused by a fast moving weather pattern that suddenly appeared on the radar. The jet stream is not behaving according to its predicted path. "Out of the blue" the jet stream took a sharp angled right turn instead of a more even keeled left one. As a result, the pilot will be required to course correct. As a necessary precaution, she requests that you store any belongings that could harm you or other passengers. You moan in discomfort and pull your seat belt to secure it more tightly around your body.

What has happened is that in a matter of minutes the pleasant and uneventful picture you had painted for your journey is quickly vanishing. Your fantasy has been interrupted by the unexpected. "Sorry folks", says the pilot. "Prepare yourself for a choppy ride." The change that has occurred was not predictable and therefore decisions will be made in the moment rather than in a step-by-step and linear manner. The pilot's previous experience, judgment and instincts will all be called into play as the flight proceeds.

The turbulence begins and the plane is tossing like a toy boat caught in rough seas. Instinctively, you know that this is only the beginning. Your heart is palpitating and you can feel the beads of perspiration forming on your upper lip. You don't want to show it, but you are afraid. You notice your fellow passengers are looking around and, as you turn in your seat, someone catches your eye. You smile and nod your head, feeling somewhat comforted that you are not alone in this situation. Nearly everyone is feeling the same at this point in the journey.

Nonetheless, the plane continues to rock and you have no idea how long the disruptive and uncomfortable turbulence will last. The only recourse you have is to remain calm and focus on a positive outcome.

SURVIVAL

What has been described in the prior scenario is the type of situation leaders can and do encounter on a daily basis. Whether in work or life, change arrives unannounced. Strong and unexpected turbulence can quickly interrupt ones world. Something changes and decisive and quick action is necessary.

Now and then, not only are external changes disturbing the natural flow of events, but at times our core foundation is challenged as well. The beliefs, perceptions and assumptions that have served us well can prove useless in the face of sudden, unexpected and unforeseen intrusion into the routines of our daily lives.

But wait a moment. In the airplane scenario described, you were a helpless and passive passenger strapped into the chair, feeling out of control and powerless, hoping the pilot is experienced enough to get through the storm safely.

Isn't this a book about leadership? In this story shouldn't you, the aspiring leader, be sitting next to the pilot, learning and observing so you will know how to deal with emergency situations?

That would have been a book about yesterday.

THIS IS A BOOK ABOUT TODAY AND THE FUTURE!

TODAY'S WORLD

We live in a complex world filled with uncertainty that creates an abundance of confusion and doubt concerning one's ability to safely navigate the rough terrain. There will be situations when reflection, careful analysis and research will need to be placed aside. Although risky, taking quick action is sometimes the only sensible solution. How you prepare and what you learn on a continuous basis can make the difference between success and failure.

As in the scenario involving the pilot and passenger in the previous story, those aspiring to be in leadership in life will need to seize the opportunity to shift from being the passive passenger to the pilot in command. Oftentimes, there is no invitation to such a task.

And that is how it's done, without months and years of preparation, observing and practicing based on the actions, guidance, advice and wisdom of others. You find yourself in charge. As you frantically seek answers in "leaders" and bemoan the fact that a roadmap wasn't handed to you, the realization that "tag, you're it" has occurred.

There are very few, if any, "apprenticeship" situations for aspiring leaders. Perhaps there never were those opportunities available to the majority who were expected to accept their lot in life. Instead they were set on a course of following the lead of others, accepting direction, and doing what they were told.

If you choose to set your own course and direction for your future, you will need to sidestep the meticulous, organized process of growing into a sheltered leadership position reserved for a few and incur the cost and risks of learning and developing your capacity as the leader in your life.

Whether you are a leader of "one" that is yourself, or a leader in your family, community or work situation, the fundamentals rarely change. The point is that having a mindset of being a leader impacts our perspective on life, communicates our value and increases our overall sense of confidence and well-being. Why wouldn't it? Once equipped for the self-designated role of "being a leader", an individual quickly grasps that learning is a lifetime activity and is incorporated easily and effortlessly in every action, decision and choice. You are in charge of your life. You learn, grow and evolve every day. You are responsible, passionate and committed to who you want to be, what you desire and how you will achieve what you want in life. Effective tools and strategies will assist you as you problem-solve and implement decisions whether as a student, entrepreneur or member of a team, group or community.

You may be the leader in an authority role or an aspiring leader. Knowledge is your power and it must be constantly replenished as the world changes every day. New technologies, new challenges await the individual taking up the calling of being a leader in life and work. Preparation is key. Effective implementation and reflecting on what was learned is an imperative.

TOMORROW'S FUTURE

Time after time in speaking, training and coaching individuals who aspire to be in leadership in life, this writer has found that if there was one single aspect each had in common it was the desire to have an impact, make a contribution, and leave a legacy no matter how great or small.

Rarely does the individual talk about a material legacy but rather an ideal, a history of accomplishment based on a personal vision, a core belief or set of values that dictate they blaze a new trail. In some instances it involves setting out far from home to begin a new life and achieving deeds that were not approachable for their parents or grandparents. Or, in some cases, the individual decides they wanted to create goals on their terms and not those set by others such as the family, social institutions or business organizations.

Frequently they gladly offered time and resources to those who had a similar quest. They were eager to share what they learned and happy to know that others wanted to discover new talents or open up new opportunities for themselves and others.

In terms of achieving their goals, in life and in work, their desire was and is to have an impact on the social environment in which they live and for a future generation.

What is your "impact" going to be?

What is it that you want to achieve that will live beyond your time here and have an impact on your world?

BEING A DELIBERATE CREATOR

Take a look at the people you admire most. Do an internet search. Find out what they do, what groups they belong to, what they share about themselves. Ask yourself what you like about them and what it is you can do RIGHT NOW to begin meeting people like them.

Brainstorm a list of areas where you want to make a difference or a contribution of time and energy.

Write it down and include a few goals you want to accomplish.

MAKING A POSITIVE DIFFERENCE MEANS BEING A DELIBERATE CREATOR.

Be a student of the world around you.
Know it.
Formulate a unique opinion and be able to express it in a compelling way.
Have passion.
Be compassionate
Have the courage to stand out on the limb alone.
Risk more.
Be more than you ever thought possible.

Unless the ground is fertile nothing will grow or it will die an early death before it gets a chance to blossom.Every living creation on the planet leaves behind some residue of their visit. Whether that is a footprint in the sand or a human being leaving a legacy for future generations, a work of art, or having helped another. For better or worse, everyone is having an impact on the society and environment in which they live.

An individual's impact is the sum total of their life's purpose, mission, or work regardless of how great or small. The very fact that they existed leaves, in their absence, an imprint.

This book is about the impact or legacy of your having lived. It's focus is on assisting you in taking stock of who you are, what you are doing, why you are here and what difference or impact your life will have had far beyond the time when you have physically existed.

The result of your leadership aspiration is your "impact".

MAKING A POSITIVE DIFFERENCE AS A DELIBERATE CREATOR MEANS MAKING RAPID CHANGE HAPPEN

NO MATTER HOW IT HAPPENS, THE PROCESS IS THE SAME.

You are changing jobs…

You have recently graduated from high school, college or graduate school…

You are frustrated with your current situation and want a change…

You want to be an entrepreneur…

You want to do work that is more meaningful…

Most of the time, the urge to make a change or take a different course or path in life is when we are most open to considering our options. Rarely, however, do people take time to think about what got them to their current state. Oftentimes, without a careful consideration of the present and past, the cycle repeats itself and they wind up back where they were.

Why is that the case?

Simply, we haven't been trained to think critically.

How is that done?

Before you become locked into a role or particular responsibility that is difficult to change, you can consider the various paths available. Depending upon your level of curiosity, determination, stamina, personal will and perseverance life will feel like a burden to bear, a minefield of problems, or an opportunity to get the results you want.

Most people will take the less stressful path and ask friends or family for their opinions and advice. They would hesitate to step onto the path single-handedly without assurances and a firm safety net. Although nets in life tend to be illusory and temporary, people strive for stability and comfort. Unless you are in a small percentage of the population who are outliers and natural born risk-takers.

Anyone who has had the honor, privilege or opportunity to coach or mentor a more junior individual just starting out on their job, career or chosen profession would agree that on more than one occasion they've had to caution the individual about following the advice of another. Yes, you can seek guidance, ask for feedback and access to resources, and listen to an experienced individual's stories and lessons they learned along the way.

However, in the end it is you who are the decider for your life. Not your partner, friend, neighbor, classmate or colleague at work.

Excusing yourself because of your circumstances, environment or pressure from peers does not exempt or prevent you from taking ownership of your life. At this point, taking ownership of your self is not about morality or judgment of good versus bad. First and foremost, it is a decision, conscious and willful, to be the sole authority over your own self that includes your body, mind, spirit and attitude.

Consider the following dialogue between John and Mary.

Mary: Why did you make those particular choices or decide on a particular course of action?

John: I chose to make those decisions based on my own research and what's important to me.

Mary: Weren't you afraid of making a mistake?

John: No I wasn't. I'm responsible for the outcome of my actions and attitudes, not anyone or anything else.

Mary: I heard it didn't turn out so well for you. Don't you feel terrible about it?

John: I don't feel badly about it. I learned a great deal and now I'm going to use that knowledge to try a new approach.

That is what an individual who is a leader in their life would say and that is how they would respond to another's inquiry into their actions or activities. Decisions were made and paths taken. It couldn't be simpler than that.

There are few if any shortcuts on this path as many will report. On some days only disappointment and frustration will be the reward. Doubt will trigger fear and anxiety, eventually leading to confusion. But never must apathy or inertia enter the picture. Even when there is uncertainty, taking action is important.

There are individuals who sleep twenty hours every day.

They are dead to the world and this is a state of being which is very difficult to correct once entangled in its deadly web. It is not impossible but it is extremely difficult to recover to any semblance of normality.

There are individuals who grope their way through every day and every night, wandering aimlessly, spending hours on the web and social media.

How did they arrive at that point in their life? It isn't difficult. They got there by existing and not living their lives in action or activities that build their sense of self worth, enjoyment of life and strong relationships.

They have little or no energy for any other person than themselves, with few inner reserves or resources to give to their families, communities or friends.

They have disappeared and are invisible to the world around them.

Are you invisible to the world around you?

MAKING A POSITIVE DIFFERENCE AS A DELIBERATE CREATOR OF RAPID CHANGE MEANS YOU NEED TO BE VISIBLE

IN WHAT WAYS ARE YOU INVISIBLE TO YOUR WORLD?

WHAT WILL YOU NEED TO DO TO CHANGE THAT CONDITION?

MAKING A POSITIVE DIFFERENCE AND CREATING RAPID CHANGE AS A VISIBLE LEADER MEANS YOU NEED TO PROMOTE YOUR BEST TRAITS

Ask friends what they think are your best traits or talents and how that shows up in conversations, actions and activities.

Look for people who are visible to the world. Find out what they are doing and how they are doing it.

Reach out to people you admire and tell them you are interviewing individuals you most admire. Ask them questions. Learn about how they think.

Incorporate what you learned into your vision-action-reality plan.

RULES FOR THE JOURNEY

MAKING A POSITIVE DIFFERENCE AS A VISIBLE LEADER AND DELIBERATE CREATOR OF RAPID CHANGE

RULES NEED TO BE UPDATED AND REVISITED ON A TIMELY BASIS

RULES NEED TO REFLECT YOUR CURRENT DESIRED STATE IN LIFE

RULES CHANGE AS LIFE AND THINGS CHANGE

MOST IMPORTANT RULE. NOTHING IS PERMANENT

THE RULES

ONE: **Assess Your Current Reality and Map Your Territory**

TWO: **Understand and Be Able and Ready to Articulate Your Value**

THREE: **Take Charge of Your Own Life and Be a Creator**

FOUR: **Develop and Build High Levels of Self-Awareness**

FIVE: **Have and Exert Influence**

SIX: **Prepare for Leadership**

SEVEN: **Develop Leadership Capacity**

EIGHT: **Declare Your Values**

NINE: **Use Your Values as Catalyst for Positive Impact**

TEN: **Know Yourself**

ELEVEN: **Be a Visible and Deliberate Creator of Rapid Change**

TWELVE: **Present Your Best Self**

RULE NUMBER ONE: ASSESS YOUR CURRENT REALITY AND MAP YOUR TERRITORY

There are reasons why you must continually reappraise your situation. Nothing is permanent and things change. Assess the current reality and map a viable path forward.

Ask yourself:

Are you the leader of your life? If not you, then who is? Can you live a life where, at every turn, you must ask someone else for the answers to your questions or critical life-changing decisions?

The question "What do you think I should do" should only be asked after you have done your own research and can intelligently share what it is you would like to know more about. Seek clarity and understanding versus opinions.

Asking another human being, "What should I do?" is an act of transferring the responsibility of decision making onto their shoulders. It is not a fair question. The person doesn't know or understand your circumstances, financial situation, talents, how you think, and what resources you have in order to provide you with a good answer.

It's challenging to convince people that the journey is best taken with a near empty satchel, curiosity to learn, testing and experimenting while creating an individualized approach to their lives.

Think of yourself as a marathon runner. You are competing with your own best self. Looking around to see where everyone else is in the race is a waste of time and energy. It is difficult to maintain focus while worrying about who or what is gaining ground on you.

We are not suggesting a grandiose plan or encouraging delusional thinking. Rather, it is about being an individual who is responsible, committed and attuned to the course of action they must take and a realistic assessment of what a good and meaningful life means. Their measure of success is counted only by themselves and based upon their own standards. Society and culture will change with the times. American culture in particular changes more rapidly than others. To name a few, there have been the roaring twenties, beatniks, hippies, yuppies, hip-hop, goth and many other cultural movements each with their own mode of dress, language and attitudes toward life. Movies, books and art provide insight into each of them revealing the values embraced by multitudes of people during that particular time period.

But what do all of those popular fads and trends mean for individual character, values, beliefs and goals?

Should the individual personality, motivations, desires and attitudes be based upon the culture of the time or is it more prudent to set the standards and live by solid principles built over a lifetime of experience, knowledge and wisdom?

These are a few of the questions you may want to consider as you ponder the bigger challenges of:

Who am I?

What am I passionate about and would commit my entire life toward achieving?

What roles describe me?

Consider:

> Disruptor
> Champion
> Catalyst
> Shaper

Shifter
Sherpa
Influencer
Connector
Change Agent
Initiator
Implementer
Problem-Solver

What is my true sense of self worth and how do I maintain my values over the course of time?

Some may find that as a result of circumstances and events, their values are not popular. Does this mean they should change? When is change required to avoid being labeled "rigid" and "out of touch with reality"? Ponder these questions for yourself.

Are you coachable? Teachable? When is adaptation the prudent path of action? When is it better to follow in the footsteps of someone who has achieved mastery in an area of excellence you wish to attain? Once again, weighty questions that can only be reconciled in a leader's own mind.

RULE NUMBER TWO: UNDERSTAND AND BE ABLE TO ARTICULATE YOUR VALUE

Every day there are stories of the rise and fall of celebrities, politicians, heads-of-state, dictators and superstars of the business world.

Reflect for a moment on an individual who rose to great heights in their professions only to end their lives with drugs, alcohol, and suicide. It isn't difficult to easily identify a few of the more well known examples.

A reasoning person might ask, "Why, if they had it all, would they ruin their lives and that of their families?"

Maybe we should question the reasons why these superstars are so revered in the first place? Did they possess an individual identity, carved out of their own desires, talents, motivations and needs? Or, were they like the moths drawn toward the flame and burned themselves out for the glory of mass adulation?

Is that leadership? In the last century it was.

For the next generation of leadership there is a different kind of thinking going on. Many don't want to be associated with the word "leader". It's seen as corrupt, immoral, power hungry, dominating, competitive, aggressive, ruthless and sometimes cruel.

Are they role-models for a life well-lived with meaning, purpose, achievement and prosperity? People who disrupt whole industries, initiate actions to feed more people, pollute less, educate in new and exciting ways, innovate empowering ways of working and sharing profit.

Did they create themselves or did someone or something else do the work for them? What was the cost and what price did they pay? Was it easy?

If you are not already there, what can be learned from these "new leaders" for a new generation of inspiring, empowering, passionate and committed individuals who challenge the status quo, take risks, make sacrifices and pay the price associated with taking stands and being bold?

What exactly does it mean to be a self-created individual in a time when being socially popular and politically correct is the norm?

How do you reconcile the need to be recognized, "liked", and "followed" with the sometimes unpopular task of being opposed to someone's idea, of a different opinion than friends or colleagues, visionary, an "out of the box" thinker, or "different from family members?

Who and what determines the measure of your worth as an individual?

The word leader is not the problem. It's what we, in previous generations wanted, asked for or accepted as the "norm". The next new generation is not aspiring to be the kind of leader that demands, commands and controls others.

Whether called leader, change agent, facilitator, or collaborator, some attributes are timeless.

In the new way of looking at leadership, it is fluid, self-directed, facilitative, collaborative, and shared.

Entrepreneurs partner, co-create, share leadership to set vision, forecast and project, innovate, disrupt, create and get the job done through planning, organizing, prioritizing, educating new talent, growing and evolving.

Perhaps this is where you aspire to be. A role-model, mentor, coach, or difference maker require significant amounts of focus, clarity, purpose, skills and certain attributes. Key among them are self-determination, self-responsibility and commitment. If you don't call yourself a leader of others, you will need to be the leader of your own life. The core of who you are is what inspires others confidence and willingness to listen to you and absorb what knowledge or guidance you are sharing. Otherwise, how will you influence, connect, build a network, acquire meaningful work, enjoy life without utilizing the skills of being a leader?

RULE NUMBER THREE: TAKE CHARGE AND OWN YOUR LIFE

Ultimately, who and what we become in our lives is within our control in spite of the circumstances and situations we grow up in, live in and work in.

It can be an enormous struggle to push back history and a society or culture that has told us otherwise.

What do you believe is within your control in life?

What do you believe is not within your control?

Based on your responses what you have left are your:

Attitude
Body language
Tone of voice
Speech
Style of dress
Mannerisms
Posture
Desires

What you have left is what is within your control.

RULE NUMBER FOUR: DEVELOP HIGH LEVELS OF SELF-AWARENESS

RULE NUMBER FIVE: HAVE AND EXERT INFLUENCE

Consider where you have influence right now.

Ask yourself where it is you would like to have more influence.

> Is it within your control?

If not, how can you explore opportunities to broaden your sphere of influence?

> Who do you know who has a sphere of influence that you admire?

Set up an interview with the individual and ask them your questions.

Incorporate your answers into your Plan.

Who are you?

Is it time for you to awaken to the potential within you, no matter who you now think you are, what you think you have or what you believe you are capable of achieving?

RULE NUMBER SIX: PREPARE FOR LEADERSHIP

As with most journeys, there is a greater chance for success when there is preparation and practice.

Important questions:

>   What works?
>   What doesn't work?
>   What needs to happen next?

The answers to these questions need to be a priority in any activity that is important to the mission.

Setting goals, planning and determining the best course of action is a wise place to begin any change.

There is a difference between preparing for an event and embarking on a journey.

>   An event is a short-term trip that has a beginning, middle and end.

>   A journey takes place over a longer period of time and is a never-ending process of learning, growing and doing.

RULE NUMBER SEVEN: DEVELOP LEADERSHIP CAPACITY

On the journey toward being a leader, it is essential that you build a solid foundation in four areas of importance to you as a whole person:

Mental
Emotional
Physical
Spiritual

Why is this important?

Because as you progress toward developing leadership, the challenges will grow in intensity and you will need to be a stronger person to meet them.

What does being strong mean?

A strong person is someone who can weather storms because they have prepared and made provision for them.

A strong person is someone who has built their willpower and courage by taking on more difficult tasks.

Equipped with sufficient and increasing amounts of knowledge and experience including habits, skills, characteristics of personality, values and goals will provide a safety net when the inevitable fall occurs.

Why is it inevitable, you might ask?

Because life consists of numerous breakdowns and breakthroughs. If you decide you want to create substantial impact in your life's journey, it is inevitable that you will fail to achieve certain milestones and goals. Change involves learning and in turn, making mistakes, uncovering weaknesses and encountering obstacles is part of the process.

Ask individuals who have achieved their desires. They will share with you that it took many attempts and there were times when they thought they would never see a positive outcome.

What made the difference for them?

They say it was failing early in the journey. They learned hard lessons. As a result, they felt more confident and focused and continued on the path more determined and wiser than they were before they started.

One step at a time. Sometimes taking leaps of faith and rapidly moving in another direction altogether. Always testing, pivoting to a new spot. Taking new actions and experimenting.

Regardless, the temptation to give up the goal in the form of lightening the load with something easier, more comfortable or safer will present itself.

But if courage, tenacity, perseverance, confidence and stamina have been building inside you, you will have what it takes to continue with your goals.

Practice is essential and all of the small failures you will experience along the way will build your fortitude as you are tested. And as you grow and evolve, you will learn and you will continue to learn and begin to see this as a natural process and a way of life.

With all goals and visions there are tests.

The difference between success and failure will be how well prepared you are to persevere and how your mindset and attitude will boost you or hinder you.

What resources do you have in place before you begin the journey of developing leadership?

Be prepared for the risks involved is essential but don't let it paralyze you into not taking action. Act despite not having all the answers. You will never know all there is to know. Otherwise, you wouldn't be changing, growing, evolving and learning. You would be sitting still watching the traffic light move back and forth between green, yellow and red. Momentum is key. Velocity is essential. Move forward with purpose, confident you will have what it takes to meet the challenges ahead.

RULE NUMBER EIGHT:
DECLARE YOUR VALUES

Consider this list of VALUES:

> Power
> Commitment
> Passion
> Responsibility
> Accountability
> Perseverance
> Courage
> Tenacity
> Integrity
> Compassion
> Love
> Respect
> Curiosity

Which VALUES hold the most meaning for you?

Which ones do you need to learn more about and build upon?

The values you choose will sustain you over the course of your journey. They will provide strength and build your stamina, tolerance, patience and ability to take the risks necessary to achieve your desires. They will be your companion, guidepost and lighthouse if and when you are standing alone, feeling isolated or confused and uncertain.

RULE NUMBER NINE: USE YOUR VALUES AS CATALYST FOR POSITIVE IMPACT

Your values will act as catalysts, motivators and life support when you need the confidence, tenacity, courage, and perseverance to move forward with your vision.

Examine where or why you came to have the values you have now. Should they change?

If so, identify what they mean to you and create a few scenarios where you will rely upon them for sustenance.

RULE NUMBER TEN: KNOW YOURSELF

How did you get to be who you are today and how did you arrive at your core beliefs about life?

Most people will walk through their entire lives without asking themselves this question or never attempt to discover who they are outside of what they were told or what others expect of them.

But as you consider forging a leadership identity, you will find it very difficult to avoid the question.

RULE NUMBER ELEVEN: BE A VISIBLE AND DELIBERATE CREATOR OF RAPID CHANGE

There are numerous books and movies that present characters with well-defined values. Carefully choose what you read and watch. You will be influenced by what you experience.

RULE NUMBER TWELVE: PRESENT YOUR BEST SELF

How prepared are you for this journey?

Do the work. Witness the results.

BEGIN NOW.

Identify an individual, a Learning Partner, you know and trust who can interview you using the following questions.

> Are you showing up as an authentic, powerful, self-confident individual who is committed to the work of developing leadership?

> Who do you admire most and why? What traits, principles, values and actions do those people portray that you respect?

> How would you describe yourself if asked to limit your answer to three words?

> What do people count on you for?

> What would you like people to say about you?

> What do you like most about yourself?

> What do you like least about yourself?

> What would you like to change about yourself?

> Where, how, and when do you feel the best about yourself?

Rate and score how well you think you did.

(Use a scale of one to five; with five being the highest.)

Ask the Interviewer to rate and score how well they think you did.

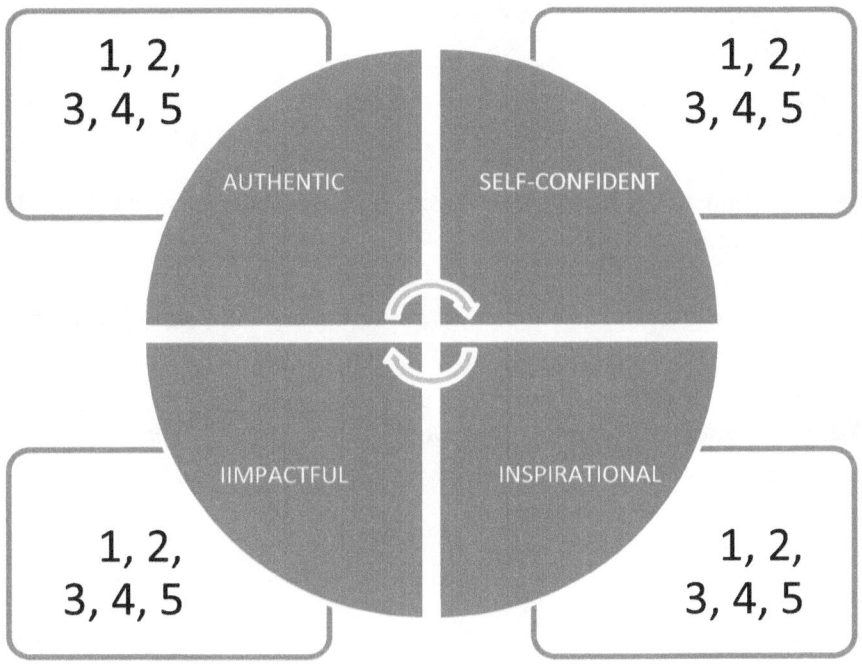

What are the differences between your self-reported scores and those of your Interviewer?

Based on those differences where do you need to improve and in what ways?

Unless we ask for specific feedback we seldom know the impact we are having on another individual.

RULE NUMBER THIRTEEN: PRESENT YOUR BEST ATTRIBUTES

Use the diagram to fill in other attributes such as committed, responsible, empowering and others.

Repeat the activity from time to time.

Use the opportunity to empower your Learning Partner to conduct the same evaluation.

Brainstorm different ways to enhance your scores and share ideas with your Interviewer.

Ask your Learning Partner if they would like to provide feedback and/or peer-to-peer coaching.

RULE NUMBER FOURTEEN: KNOW YOUR CURRENT STATE

Assess your current state:

What are you doing right now that is forwarding your vision?

How are you feeling about who you are being and what you are doing?

What are you thinking? Are your thoughts empowering and inspiring you?

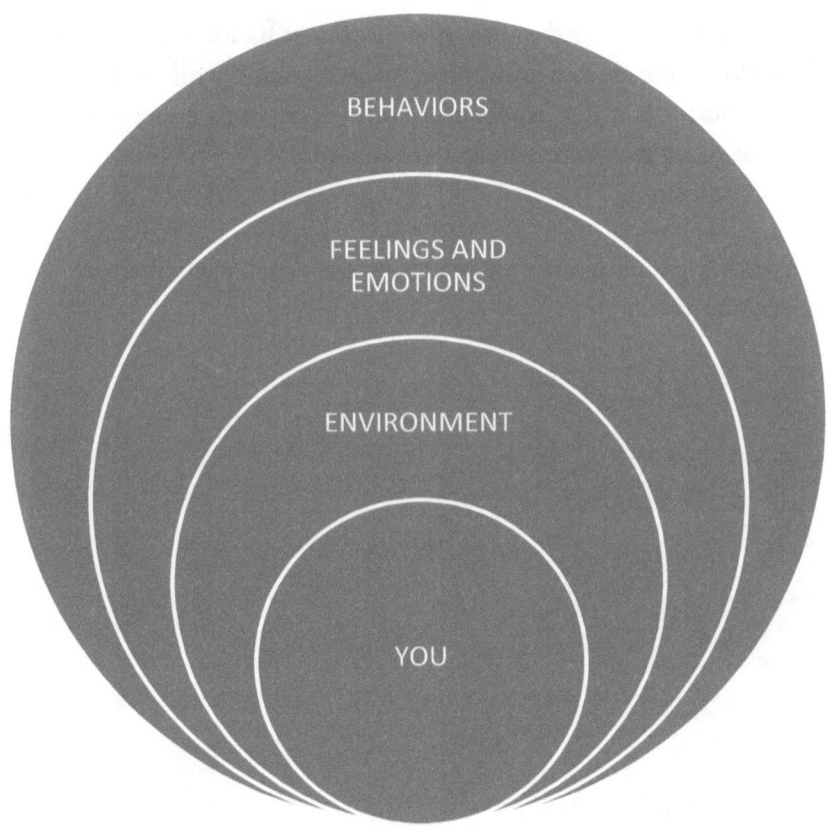

WHAT IS YOUR CURRENT REALITY? WHATEVER IT IS, IT WILL EITHER OPEN UP MORE OPPORTUNITIES OR CREATE OBSTACLES.

Now it is time to hit the pause button in your brain and take a few moments to reflect on your current situation or reality.

Questions can act as powerful triggers to help you explore what may be unexamined areas of your thinking process. Rather than shutting off the mind with repetitive mantras or entertainment, use questions to stimulate and empower yourself.

A leader is always focused on the present task at hand, while also looking and thinking ahead. Learning how to be strategic while implementing essential tactics is a key leadership ability and must be cultivated. It's important to know where you are strong and where you are weak in this area of competence.

Begin with an examination of who you are, what you value and what's important to you.

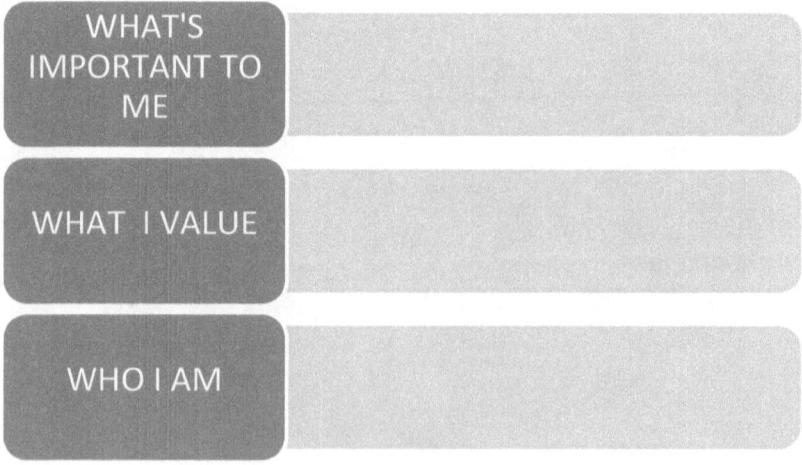

Jo Singel

RULE NUMBER FIFTEEN: KNOW YOUR BELIEFS AND ATTITUDES

... AS THEY DEFINE YOU AND YOUR DESTINY

USE THE OPPORTUNITY TO ENLIST YOUR LEARNING PARTNER, GOOD FRIEND OR COLLEAGUE TO DISCUSS THE FOLLOWING QUESTIONS WITH YOU.

> Do you know why you believe certain things to be true? Such as who you trust and why, what you believe is in your control and what is not, how you define a good life.
>
> Is it because someone taught you what you know or have you carefully examined your responses, attitudes and behaviors?

For example, people engage in relationships which result in unfulfilling situations.

People marry, take on partners, have children and grow into old age feeling angry, dissatisfied, frustrated and confused.

They look around at their life's circumstances and feel regret, sadness and even indignation and resentment toward their loved ones.

Or, there are people who work very hard at their jobs, battling every day to win promotions, move up in their careers only to get to retirement age and wonder where all the years have gone.

There is little or no sense of achievement or accomplishment, only a pension and a monetary nest egg.

RULE NUMBER SIXTEEN: BUILD YOUR COURAGE MUSCLES

Use the following questions as discussion points with those you care about. Build your courage muscles with your openness to feedback and hearing other people's ideas and feelings.

What is your current attitude toward life?

Does life feel like a burden to bear, a minefield of problems or an opportunity to achieve what you want?

Do you feel caught in the drift of life or are you in charge of your emotions?

What circumstances led you to this particular point of view?

What people, places and things were involved and over what period of time?

Do you use moments, hours, days, months, decades to measure your lifespan and calculate its quality?

What do you want to leave as your legacy?

CREATE A "LIFE STORY TIMELINE"

BUILD A CHRONICLE OF EVENTS THAT INCLUDE PEOPLE, PLACES AND THINGS THAT HAVE HAD AN IMPACT ON YOU.

Take a clean, white sheet of unlined paper and proceed to draw a line horizontally across the middle of the sheet. (If you choose, you can create a special notebook for updates to your Life Story Timeline. The exercises in the book will ask you to record insights, action plans, goals and visions as we proceed with the work ahead.) This line will represent your life span that will comprise an overview of the people, places, events and things in your life – from birth to death.

Mark off increments of between five and ten years, spanning the beginning of your life to the end of your life.

Now, place significant events such as births, deaths, celebrations, graduations or other life-altering occasions on the line. Project out into the future of your life. Where will you be? What events have taken place? What projects have been completed or goals fulfilled? Place each one on the line.

Take a step back and examine what you've determined are the most significant events that have occurred to you over the course of your life.

Identify important and significant relationships that you have had in your life. Place them on your line and indicate when you met those particular individuals or groups and when you may have broken off relationships with them.

You are now prepared to identify and analyze patterns. Can you see trends or make connections in between events? Did certain people, situations or things create triggers for future events? Can you see any clear "cause and effect" scenarios?

Now is the time to reflect upon what you have considered up until this point to be true for your life and what possibilities are yet to be explored.

"LIFE STORY TIMELINE" REVIEW

Work with a Learning Partner to discuss your Life Story Timeline.

Encourage your Learning Partner to create one of their own.

Use the following questions to have a powerful conversation that matters to both of you.

> What does your Life Story Timeline say about you and your desired state of being? What is missing, if anything? What has brought you joy, satisfaction and fulfillment? Consider how you can use that energy to create more of what you desire in life. It can be a powerful motivator for continuing the journey of learning, growing and evolving both personally and professionally.

> How satisfied are you with your sense of power, presence, self-esteem and personal action plan for obtaining necessary feedback on the values you are living?

Jo Singel

USE YOUR "LIFE STORY TIMELINE" AS A POWERFUL TOOL

The Life Story Timeline is a perfect tool for assessing the following:

Where am I now?

How did I get here?

Is this where I want to be?

If not, how and what changes are required as a course of action?

What can I project about the future based on where I am right now?

Is there sufficient motivation to continue the path of learning, growing and evolving?

Are there sufficient levels of velocity and momentum for change?

As a result of this activity you will be in a better position to continue a personal inquiry into how you arrived at your current state.

Share your story with a trusted friend or colleague and enlist them in the idea of creating one of their own.

Through conversation, discuss the various high and low points and ways in which you can learn, grow and evolve as a result of them. This tool can be used for team initiative implementations, career review and can be modified for individual performance activities.

RULE NUMBER SEVENTEEN: KNOW WHAT YOU WANT AND WHY IT IS IMPORTANT

What is the price you are willing to pay to get there? There are costs to everything in life. Time, energy, focus. attention and postponement of certain activities. Make your vision for your life big enough that your motivation will propel you to achieve your potential and contribute your gifts and talents to benefit yourself and those you care about.

RULE NUMBER EIGHTEEN: REMOVE THE BAGGAGE AND CREATE BREATHING SPACE

Our baggage is the stories we tell ourselves about why we can't achieve what we want. Fear, anger, lack of self-confidence, remorse, guilt, holding on to stale jobs, relationships and things that don't represent who we are or who we want to be.

Imagine that the sum total of your entire history is stored in a large closet. Visualize what might be stored there.

Based on what you see or sense is currently stored in the closet, what are you actually using? Conversely, what is being stored that you haven't used in a very long time? What has been tossed to the back of the closet and until now has remained unnoticed, forgotten and gathering dust? Talents you didn't nurture? Knowledge you acquired and didn't use?

Understand that it takes courage to open up the closets of unexamined beliefs, assumptions and the experiences of our lives. We can never know what we will find unless we take the first step to look. Beliefs about being a leader, not having enough education, not having what it takes to pursue your dreams.

Attempt to set aside some of the mind chatter of accusations and judgments.

It isn't necessary to identify excuses, reasons and stories for past behaviors. It was the best choice you had available to you at the time.

It's difficult to discard things that cause feelings of remorse, shame or embarrassment and instead we tell ourselves, "Well, maybe someday I'll use it. Better keep it here in the closet but push it further to the back or wrap it up in plastic so when I need it, it will not be riddled with moth holes."

Try not to be tempted to salvage the past. It is of no use or value to you now. You already paid the price for it, no point in paying for it again. It would be futile to attempt to justify past choices and decisions. The mental activity only serves to keep you locked into the past when you took the action that made the most sense. It is in the present that you have an opportunity to make new choices based on a fresh perspective and different experiences.

RULE NUMBER NINETEEN: RELEASE THE PAST

...AS IT WILL HINDER YOUR FUTURE FROM OCCURRING AS YOU WANT IT TO.

Brainstorm the question:

> What do I need to discard from the past that no longer serves me?

Answer the questions:

> Now what?

> What's next?

The task of re-creation always begins with the self.

- Jo Singel

RULE NUMBER TWENTY: BE AN INDIVIDUAL OF YOUR OWN DESIGN AND DESIRE

WHO AND WHAT DEFINES YOU HAS THE LAST WORD. It takes time, work, perseverance, courage, and fortitude to acquire the competencies, traits, attitudes and abilities needed for a desired future. Wanting to be a leader in life and not just at work or in the community is a big commitment and requires discipline and focus.

How did you come to be who you are right now?

What's working in your life?

What's not working in your life?

Are there people, places or things you need to let go of?

Oftentimes, we fail to let go of people, places and things that no longer serve us or our vision.

What are you holding onto and for what reasons? What is the worst case scenario if you let go? Imagine your daily life without those things. How would you feel? Are you afraid there is nothing to replace them?

Being in a state of leadership in life allows for more choices and possibilities. Learning, growing and evolving disrupts the status quo and all that we became comfortable thinking, doing and feeling. Now, at this point of the journey, new learning may feel uncomfortable. This is the time to reinforce what you desire and create a vision for your life that is big and so powerful that it will withstand the discomfort that comes with change.

Ahead, we will explore self-awareness, habits, rules, decision-making and how we handle change. Every step of the way is an activity that works on building certain emotional muscle groups so that in the end, everything becomes more centered, balanced and stabilized for what's next. Learning while taking action at the same time builds the necessary velocity and momentum for motivation to continue.

RULE NUMBER TWENTY-ONE: BE SELF-AWARE AND REDUCE UNWELCOME SURPRISES

As in everything else that you do to create the life and work you desire, there are certain factors that will determine the difference between a life you find acceptable or one that you feel totally great about. A life that makes you eager to see the light of day after a good night's sleep. A life that causes you to leap from bed, eager to start a new day.

Learning how to develop your leadership abilities is no exception to the rule.

A critical factor in any kind of learning is awareness.

Awareness is a critical building block determining the speed at which you will be able to claim the next level of being a leader in life as well as in work. Whether working as a solopreneur, student, professional, community organizer, awareness is key to achieving meaningful outcomes.

What does awareness mean?

Awareness is not an event or a transaction.

It is:

A state of being open to new information while weighing and choosing between conflicting streams of incoming data in order to determine next moves or actions.

It is not action itself or a substitute for action.

What is required?

Attentiveness

Intent to know in order to take deliberate and focused action

Using the senses to engage with the environment

It is a place of non-action, of listening and paying attention to all that is within and around you.

BUILDING SELF-AWARENESS ACTIVITY

Visualize deer standing still in the woods, sensing what is around them and taking in information through sight, sound, feel, and smell.

Awareness, as distinguished from self-awareness is a very powerful tool to practice and possess.

What can you do to enhance your awareness skills?

Take a walk in a natural environment. Stop, look and listen to your surroundings.

What do you notice?

Spend time quietly contemplating what is around you on a daily basis without interference from external distractions.

How do you feel as a result?

> Alert?
>
> Focused?
>
> In-Tune?
>
> Clear?

Take a few moments to jot down some of your thoughts, reflections and any ideas which came to mind as you took a walk or sat back and allowed yourself to unwind.

Nearly every waking moment of modern life is filled with messages. They come from social media, families, relationships, work environments, professors and the anecdotal bits and pieces of conversations heard in public places.

Where do you get the information you need to help you form your own opinions, judge situations and determine what you think, feel and know about something?

Who do you rely upon to help you sort through the complex and sometimes confusing mass of information and data that you are bombarded with every day?

You will not find the information and knowledge you need in sound bites or other forms of social media, gossip and hearsay. You will need to sift through the mounds of information and sensory data to FIND YOUR TRUTH.

This is a critical leadership task.

It is a discovery process and due diligence is required in order to separate what is real from what is not. In an age of information overload, this is not an easy task.

RULE NUMBER TWENTY-TWO: KNOW YOUR HABITS

...AS THEY DEFINE YOUR DAILY LIFE AND IMPACT A FUTURE OF YOUR CHOICE.

Leaders must carefully examine the routines and habits they have acquired over the course of time and experience. It doesn't take long before our habits begin to define us in rigid and harsh ways. Which ones are useful and which are not? It's difficult to be fully conscious all of the time. More than likely, we would hardly accomplish anything since we spend the majority of our time analyzing information, situations and other data that overwhelm every waking moment of our lives.

Habits are those short cuts that help us cope with the minor decisions we must make every day in order to live. Ordering lunch, choosing what to wear in the morning, the time we awaken and sleep and other essential habits allow us to function with some normalcy on a daily basis.

Routines become so habitual we can hardly remember the time when we made other choices.

Not only do we go on automatic pilot with the uninteresting parts of our lives, sacrificing consciousness for the sake of convenience, we also do the same for more significant and important situations. Those are the areas that can cost in missed opportunities, lost friendships, outdated skills, untapped talents, lethargy and an overall sense of dullness. In this regard, life is a high-stakes game. How do you wish to play it? Always open to new and interesting strategies? Learning new techniques? Perfecting skills that matter?

RULE NUMBER TWENTY-THREE: GET UNSTUCK

...KNOW YOUR FEELINGS OR GET SIDETRACKED IN YOUR PROGRESS

IF YOU ARE NOT MAKING PROGRESS YOU ARE STUCK IN THE STATUS QUO. THEREFORE, YOU WILL BE, AS THEY SAY, A SITTING DUCK. The following is a list of incomplete sentences designed to spark recognition of what is a routine task and what requires your full consciousness.

> When I need to make a decision I usually...
>
> In order for me to feel good about myself, I...
>
> When confronted I usually...
>
> When I feel uncertain I...
>
> When I feel afraid I...
>
> When I have low energy I...
>
> When I feel I've been sabotaged I...

Your responses provide feedback on your habitual behaviors and routines. The list can be longer and you and your Learning Partner can brainstorm and quiz others. This is a good indicator of when you are on automatic pilot. So some things need to change? Are these habits you prefer to keep? Or do you think it is in your best interest to change some of these habits of routine behavior? Only you can decide what is right for you as an individual who is a leader in life.

HABITS EXERCISE

After identifying some of your habits, reflect on the following questions:

> Do your habits help or hinder you from achieving your goals?

> Do they push you further away or do they enable you to get what you want?

If applicable, list the habits you'd like to change and those that support your goals.

Plan for how you will go about changing them.

Create a list of short term and long term objectives and review the sentence completion exercise every few months to see what progress you are making.

RULE NUMBER TWENTY-FOUR: MAKE RULES THAT SERVE YOUR VISION

From our earliest lives, our parents or teachers tell us the rules for living. Over time, like our habits, we latch onto prescribed rules that make up the history and stories of our lives. Rules govern our results in very powerful yet subtle ways. When we have a rule about something, no matter what the context of the situation we are facing we reach out, very quickly, for the tool called "our rules".

Rules come in the form of the following:

- How we manage difficult relationships and situations
- Kinds of people we associate with
- Types of careers we engage in
- Our relationship to time
- How we treat leisure
- How we manage stress
- How we deal with loss
- How we deal with authority
- How we deal with loss of control
- How we handle conflict

RULE NUMBER TWENTY-FIVE: MAKE DECISIONS AND CHOICES THAT SERVE YOUR VISION

Rules go hand in hand with making decisions. First, we consult our rules for managing people, places, things and experiences. Most of the time, as we have reviewed, we are on automatic pilot. It makes life easier that way. As a reminder, this is a toolkit focused on developing leadership in life and, as we have been learning, the status quo is not an option.

We are replacing mindlessness with mindful behavior and strengthening our awareness in order to be more fully present to our experience, accessing more of our talents and hidden capabilities.

The following incomplete sentences can help to distinguish why you are making a certain decision and under what circumstances. If we only make certain decisions to feel good, be recognized or bolster our ego, it is a good time to examine what is involved motivationally and what drives our behavior and choices. Will our routine method of operating serve our purposes?

I feel confident when I…

I won't feel confident until…

I feel successful when I…

I'm not happy until…

I feel loved when I…

My life is going well when I…

I feel I've accomplished something when I…

My work is good when…

I feel content, satisfied and peaceful when...

IMPACTFUL RULES ACTIVITY

The following questions will help you to continue to reflect on the impact of the RULES that influence your choices and decisions.

- What has to happen (my rules are being addressed) for me to have what I want?
- Are my rules helping or hindering me in achieving my goals?
- Which rules propel me forward?
- Which rules keep me back?
- Which rules act as guide maps as I create more of what I want?
- What rules keep me stuck in the status quo?

"CHANGING THE RULES" ACTIVITY

Work with your Learning Partner and share three rules you would like to keep and three rules you'd like to change or eliminate. Articulate your reasons for the change and the impact you want this change to have on your life and work.

Record your insights and desired changes in your Life Story Timeline and see if, over time, there are any noticeable changes in the results you want to achieve. Does it change or influence your relationships, work, vision or sense of well-being and happiness?

HANDLING CHANGE ACTIVITY

No matter what age you are, life has a way of interrupting what you are doing and challenging an aspect of your life that is unexpected, unplanned and oftentimes, unwanted.

What do you do when this happens?

Most of the time, individuals react and respond in the best possible way as the interruption is occurring. What can make a difference, however, is to examine those interruptions in retrospect and learn as much as possible from them. When life interrupts again, we will have more experience and knowledge from which to gather inner strength, courage and determination to meet the challenges. We will be better equipped and prepared for the change process itself and in some ways, prosper personally, emotionally and physically as well. Still and all, there are some changes that are completely unwanted and very disruptive. In this regard, resilience, adaptiveness and agility will be enhanced by the discipline of taking time to look back in order to proceed forward with new awareness and resolve. In other words, the change does not take us down so far we cannot rise from it.

Reflect on an interruption that you had during the recent past.

What happened? Was there an event that precipitated the interruption or did it literally come at you suddenly and without warning?

- How did you respond?
- Are you pleased with how you handled the situation?
- Would you rather have reacted differently?
- What could have made a difference?

If that particular interruption happened again, how would you react in the present time?

Are there any resources or new knowledge that you need to acquire to be better prepared in the future?

What lesson did you learn from the interruption? Perhaps you learned a valuable lesson and have now incorporated it into your life. It's important to take time to reflect on these experiences. Think how you might incorporate the lesson in a story or example when you are helping others learn similar experiences. This is the path of leadership.

DECISION-MAKING UNDER PRESSURE ACTIVITY

As the tension builds between the leaders' current challenges and present situations, new choices present themselves.

What do the choices you make under pressure say about you?

If you were the protagonist or hero/heroine in a movie, how do you react to pressure, stress, calamity, strife, injury, illness, misfortune, or accident?

As the hero/heroine in the story, people will know, based on your reactions and behavior whether you have integrity, honesty, truthfulness, courage, intelligence and cleverness to deal with challenging and sometimes, life threatening situations.

The audience would also know the quality of your character, how authentic you are or have been until that moment when you were tested.

Life always presents challenges to carefully crafted plans and visions.

How you handle yourself in times of challenge or crisis will define you as a leader.

If you've been a fake or a flake, the world will see you for who you really are. If you have intentionally deceived others they will know you for the person that was hiding behind a mask, personal charisma, and a charming personality.

The bottom line? It is your choice! Will you be silent or will you speak up, take stands and allow yourself to be vulnerable to criticism, being disliked, threatened, or viewed with disdain? Those are the prices of leadership. Leaders are not always applauded and praised for the stands they take or the strong values they strive to uphold during good times and bad. Who are you and what kind of leadership do you want to be known for?

CREATING YOUR FUTURE

Write a letter to yourself from the future.

In the space of five years from now, who are you, what are you doing and what are you most proud of?

What have you learned about yourself that had the most positive and unexpected impact?

What have you learned about others that enlightened and inspired you?

What are you most grateful for?

Who and what do you appreciate the most?

What do you want the next five years to be about?

What do you want to carry forward into the present and the future?

RULE NUMBER TWENTY-SIX: OWN YOUR DESTINY

Send the "To the Future" letter you wrote to a trusted friend and discuss insights or explore what you wrote in more detail while using anecdotal stories to provide more context. Use the letter as content and inspiration for a vision board or as part of your visioning and strategizing possible futures and goals.

> Who will you need to be over the next five years to achieve this vision of your life?

> Who and what will you need in your life to champion, support, inspire or provide guidance or mentorship?

Describe in great detail how you will feel in that future vision.

> What baggage might you need to let go of?

> What values will you most rely upon?

> What habits help you move through your daily life with ease and peacefulness?

> What rules will help you make mindful decisions and take meaningful actions?

> What symbols, images, metaphors or affirmations might help you during times of challenge?

> What will you need to learn and what new knowledge will you be expected to acquire?

How will you remain fresh, vital and focused on a future you desire?

For a well-rounded activity, include your insights into your vision board. It will make a difference.

RULE NUMBER TWENTY-SEVEN: DEVELOP PRESENCE

Have you ever noticed that certain people have an energy about them that communicates self-confidence? In emergency situations, they will quickly step out of the crowd to offer help and assistance without being asked or invited.

These individuals have presence. You can't always define presence but you can recognize or feel it. What you might observe is that a person with presence walks differently than others. There is an air of self-assuredness about them. You notice them in a crowded room. They communicate clearly, and have an attitude that conveys they can be counted on if necessary or if asked. More often than not, you won't need to request their assistance.

They'll know when to jump into a situation and either take charge or lend a hand in what needs attention. On other occasions, you'll notice the individual when they voice a concern or an opinion. They conduct themselves in such a way that others listen and take note of what they are saying. They aren't necessarily always liked or loved. They are respected. They have either quiet energy or are noticeable in their poised manner. They are deliberate and focused.

You might ask yourself:

Why is that person getting attention when they aren't in charge or sitting at the head of the table? What makes them stand out above the rest? What makes them seem different from the majority of their peers?

Where does this real and non-contrived presence arise? Presence occurs within the individual and can be expressed as:

> Will-power
> Self-control

Self-confidence
Determination
Courage
Being awake, aware and alert

Consider the relationship between personal power, attitude toward authority and possessing a powerful presence. How are they related to one another? How does one depend upon another?

RULE NUMBER TWENTY-EIGHT: COMMUNICATE FOR IMPACT

An individual who communicates presence in a powerful and confident way clearly projects that they can be relied upon. You want to know this person even if you aren't certain why.

If you observe the person's behavior carefully you will identify the following activities:

- Actively engaged, whether quietly or assertively, in their environment and what is going on around them
- Focused on what is in front of them and not having silent conversations with themselves. You clearly sense they are paying attention to their surroundings.
- Alert to what you are doing and saying while simultaneously remaining tuned into the environment around them.
- Engaged in multi-tasking but treating each task discreetly and with great finesse and poise.
- Communicating their willingness and desire to show up in life through action.

An individual possessing presence is enthusiastic and interested in people and what is taking place around them. Curiosity, openness, flexibility and eagerness are often used to describe a person with real, trustworthy presence.

An individual with presence will exhibit certain kinds of behaviors and act in particular ways that can be clearly observed.

You will notice them involved when they are engaged in the following activities:

Reacting in an emergency to help others without being asked or assigned a role.

Initiating improvements and following through on the idea.

Taking the initiative in a project whether at home, school or work.

Calling attention to wrongdoing.

Encouraging others to achieve their goals.

Speaking passionately about what they believe and value.

Energetically getting involved in whatever it is they say they are committed to.

Offering assistance without a specific invitation.

Questioning or challenging the reasons why something is being done in a certain way.

RULE NUMBER TWENTY-NINE: BE SELF-CONFIDENT

Without a belief in self a leader is like a ship without a rudder and is prone to adopting what is expedient and not necessarily what is authentic and real. Pay careful attention to this particular Rule since it plays a crucial role in all of your endeavors.

Oftentimes, people become paralyzed by their situations, fears, and inhibitions because they lack the belief that they can actually have an effect on their own circumstances. They feel powerless to take action on their own behalf.

Everyone at one point in time doubts themselves. This is normal and to be expected except when it becomes a persistent state. Doubts raise questions that demand answers.

Leaders who have experienced doubt and deal with them in an honest and thoughtful way acquire compassion and empathy for others. This is the hallmark of a leader with authentic presence. Unless and until you go through the experience yourself, you cannot understand what another might be thinking and feeling.

A hallmark for effective leadership is when they are characterized by the following testimonials.

He/she is such an understanding person.

Is a good listener.

Has empathy for another's situation.

Takes time to comprehend facts and data.

Anticipates what individuals need to learn next.

Always takes the time to reward others for a job well done.

BELIEFS AND ASSUMPTIONS ACTIVITY

Take some time to reflect on your beliefs, assumptions, conditioned responses, past experiences and family legacy that have had an influence on who you are, how you act or be in the world, what you create and what you have accomplished in your life.

Question:

> Who or what has influenced your decisions and has had significant impact on your life?

Recall a time when you felt the urge tugging at you to voice an opinion that you felt would not be popular or others would not approve and you didn't share your thoughts.

> What prevented you from voicing your concern or opinion?

> Had you tried before and failed?

> Did someone attack you either verbally or physically?

> Did you feel ostracized as a result?

ASSESSING ROADBLOCKS ACTIVITY

Write down thoughts and feelings that arise as you recall the scenario that comes to mind in the last activity.

Now, rewrite the scenario in a way that has you voicing an opinion, taking a stand or sharing your thoughts and feelings.

> How do you feel as a result?
>
> What would need to be different for you to take a new action?
>
> What blocks or prevents you from moving forward?

Write in your Life Story Timeline your insights and different ways you may behave the next time you are in a situation where you have an opportunity to voice your opinion, ideas or thoughts.

RULE NUMBER THIRTY: ALWAYS BE CURIOUS

Spend time reflecting on the questions outlined in the next activity,

Use them as a guide to create your own questions. Keep inventing new and more complex questions. Question everything all the time and every day. Encourage others to question the nature of things.

Original thinking is in short supply and is rarely encouraged whether in school or at work. Be curious about yourself and others. Examine different aspects of a problem or situation. Looking at things differently is a leadership skill that can be developed with time and diligent work.

This is where true power lies.

Take yourself and others seriously. Don't accept the standard answers; knock down the institutionalized and clichéd answers. Tear down the walls between you and your own truth.

Attempt to describe what you feel rather than what you think you should say regarding an answer. Get past what it is you already know and move toward a fresh perspective.

Remember that you are the decider. Your own conscience is the final arbiter of what is right and what is wrong for you and for your world.

Jo Singel

SELF-ANALYSIS ACTIVITY

Use these questions to conduct a thorough self-examination. It is a very important process. Note your responses. Take your time. It's an activity that you can use from time to time and is not meant to be completed in one sitting.

Questions of Self-Reflection

- How did I come to be who I am today? Was it by chance or accident?
- Who would I be if no one was there to tell me what I could do or where I could go?
- What is the purpose of my life?
- Are my actions a result of what others have advised me to do or based on my own judgment?
- What am I doing that I am proud of?
- What am I sorry about or regret?
- What can people count on me for?

Questions of Faith in Self

- From where do I draw my strength?
- Where do I find solace and comfort in times of strife?
- When my patience and tolerance are tested, how do I react?
- What do I reach for when I am confused, angry, in despair, lonely, or anxious? People? Material objects? Inner guidance?

Questions of Trust

- Do people seek my opinions?
- Do people turn to me in time of need?

- Do people ask me to lead activities, other people, and projects?
- Am I sought after as a person, a friend, or a neighbor?

Questions of Caring for Self and Others

- Who in my life counts on me?
- What do I do to ensure that I am healthy - financially, emotionally, psychologically and physically?

Questions of Responsibility

- Who do I blame when things go wrong?
- How do I handle disappointment and failure?
- Do I walk toward or away from risk - whether personal, financial or emotional?

CONSTRUCTIVE FEEDBACK ACTIVITY

To deeper your self-examination that you conducted in an earlier activity, focus time and attention on the activity of asking for constructive feedback. Oftentimes, people are reluctant to solicit feedback. However, with a moderate amount of structure and preparation it can be accomplished comfortably and with very productive results.

You can begin by identifying several individuals who you trust will honor your request for feedback.

Write an explanatory email, asking the individuals for a few minutes of their time. A twenty-minute meeting, structured around a set of questions which you will provide, will be required. You can provide these questions in advance so as to better facilitate a deep discussion.

> What qualities do I have, that if I did more of them, would make me more effective?
>
> What qualities do I most appreciate about myself?
>
> What is difficult about me?
>
> What part of me is difficult to get along with?
>
> How might I be limiting myself or keeping myself back from accomplishing what I know I can achieve?

ACTIVITY ON MENTORING

Send a letter of thanks to the individuals who took the time and energy to provide you with feedback. Perhaps you can offer to return the favor if they so desire. You can also share with them your leadership learning journey and if there is curiosity and interest on their part, offer to be a Learning Partner for a trial period of time. They may also be looking for a mentor or want to be a mentor. A dialogue can also deepen your conversations with individuals who, like yourself, are interested in learning, growing and evolving in their leadership.

"QUICK FEEDBACK REQUEST" ACTIVITY

Another tool with which you can successfully invite individuals to provide you with relevant and useful feedback is to ask colleagues or friends a few focused questions versus a lengthier discussion as in the previous feedback activity.

Ask for a brief meeting that can be done by phone.

As a colleague, client or business partner, what do you:

- Appreciate most about me?
- Think might be limiting me?
- Believe are my best qualities?
- Think are my strengths, talents and qualities?

The feedback you obtain in this manner can be very enlightening and provide you with valuable insights as to how your behavior is impacting those with whom you have daily and consistent contact.

Once again, thank the individuals for the time and energy. You might also offer to provide the same service to them if they think it would be helpful.

BEING A LEADER: INTRODUCTION

THE STATE OF LEADERSHIP IN TODAY'S WORLD

The world of work and life today demands a new way of thinking, being and doing. Old models will prevail until traditional ways of looking at things completely shift and change.

This will take time and a new perspective. Until that day arrives, you will need to examine and reflect upon how you will thrive, grow and be successful on your own terms, measures and standards.

There will be numerous situations when the path will not be clear.

People who are in traditional roles of authority, with power over your daily existence may not have a roadmap to share with you that suits your goals and desires. The new way of being in leadership does not come with a prescribed formula. The ingredients will consist of your own thought process, field-tested tools and a healthy dose of risk-taking and appetite for challenge. During the journey you may discover that leadership can be quiet, watchful and nearly invisible to others.

The need for leadership can arise spontaneously. Your ability to respond will depend upon your level of preparedness. There will be no one to tell you exactly what to do in a given situation. You will have to create the most appropriate path as you make the journey.

What is important to bear in mind is that leaders are not heroes performing superhuman feats. They are people who make mistakes, fail, cry, get discouraged and feel afraid. At times, they are indecisive and uncertain of the best course of action. They may whimper when hurt, get angry, feel frustration, throw temper tantrums, complain, and take more than their fair share on occasion.

The difference will be that they will know when to stop and take a different course of action and change their behavior.

DEFINING A LEADER

What is your definition of being a leader?

Does your definition of leadership come from history books? When you were growing up did your parents tell you stories of heroes and heroines? Did you gain knowledge of leaders through books or movies? Or, perhaps your favorite fictional characters who fight evil to win the good for civilization? Have you accepted as true that anyone in authority is a leader? Is your boss or manager your leader as well?

Understanding who or what means "leader or leadership" to you is key to coming to grips with this question. Strive to be an original and creative thinker on these questions. There are no right or wrong answers. However, what you think and believe will determine the quality of your life.

Identifying who and what a leader is doesn't require a particular education or skill-set.

There are numerous business books that will gladly decide for you. In so doing, however, you will probably not come up with an original thought of your own. Perhaps without realizing it, you will be influenced by another's thinking process. That is why it is important to question, research and look with a careful eye on what it is others want to convince you is the right and true path for you. Yes, you can derive good information from studying the opinions of others. Simply question them. Turn the responses over and over in your mind, poking holes and looking for gaps in their thinking and your understanding.

Ultimately, what you decide will be your own true and real guide.

Crafting a leadership identity that is uniquely yours will require patience as you seek to challenge your own thought process and how you arrive at what it is you think you know about this topic.

KINDS OF LEADERS

Some people are naturally inclined toward leadership. Early in life, they exhibit recognizable qualities, characteristics, traits, attitudes and aspirations of a leader. That may have been you or you had friends who you thought of as leaders.

Other people learn how to be leaders through the guidance of mentors, role models, teachers, parents, and others who care, are concerned and are good coaches.

Some people quietly take up the leadership challenge without fanfare or great announcements.

Still others learn slowly but with great determination through encouragement and exposure to others who are behaving consistently in ways that communicate values and principles of authentic leadership.

And ultimately, there are those who rise naturally to a place in their family, society or work where they are trusted, have credibility, are loved and seen as responsible, committed and supportive of the well-being of others. They are considered to be leaders in life.

LEARNING LEADERSHIP IS A PROCESS

Leadership is an iterative process, progression and dynamic forward movement from a state of inaction to one of actions enabled by commitment, passion, energy and enthusiasm for achieving a goal to be satisfied in the near term or future.

It is a challenge to remain committed to a process over a lengthy period of time. We live in a transactional world, moving from event to event, exchanging what we do for what we need to live. Process is uncomfortable for most people because it involves revisiting, revising and learning from what happened to inform what will or should happen next. Most individuals would prefer to transact as it's easier and faster.

Not every situation in life requires a process to unfold or evolve. However, for long lasting achievement, process is the surest method to deliver the most positive results.

Leadership, as a process, is not an event to be achieved. Rather, leadership is a steady, firm, disciplined and multi-faceted commitment with results achieved over time and applied situation by situation.

WHAT LEADERSHIP IS NOT

As important as it is to understand what leadership is, it's equally critical to identify what it is not.

When you have observed these behaviors in others, how does it make you feel?

Bullying

Aggression

Intimidation

Abuse of power

Need to control others

Cynicism

Pessimistic about people and life

Laziness

Lack of energy or enthusiasm

Lack of concern for others

Being narrow-minded

Antagonistic

As a leader, would you want to have others feel the way you just felt? Be aware of your behaviors and their impact on others.

"BEHAVIOR FEEDBACK" ACTIVITY

Discuss with a trusted friend your responses to the following questions:

What attributes or behaviors have you engaged in that have been offensive to others?

What do you need to do in order to address the issues you may have with stubbornness, willfulness, cynicism and other traits that will prevent you from achieving your leadership aspiration in an enlightening and empowering way?

"TAKING INITIATIVE" ACTIVITY

Have you ever noticed, whether in yourself or in observing others, how easy it is to keep a low profile and wait for someone else to take the lead in an activity or project?

How would you like to change this, or help others to change this attitude and behavior?

"SELF-EMPOWERMENT" ACTIVITY

If you find yourself in a place of inertia, low energy, lacking in passion and commitment to a **goal, consider** the following:

- How many times on a daily basis do you stifle your own opinion about a topic or situation?
- How many times do you check in with friends or family, gathering advice and opinions?
- How many times do you override your own instincts and follow the judgments of another?
- How many times have you wished you had taken more risks for what it is you want in life?
- How often do you take the time to sit down and consider your next course of action based on your chosen goals?

Based on how you currently feel and your responses to the above questions, evaluate whether or not a change in attitude or behavior is necessary at this point in time.

If so, consult with your Learning Partner and devise some strategies to help make a difference in attitude, self-esteem and self-worth. Taking certain stands, such as seeing yourself as a Contributor, Thought Leader, Mentor, Initiator, Influencer, Problem-Solver, Innovator, Strategist, Idea person, Maker or other role. Work on exhibiting these qualities, skills and behaviors.

You can shift the dynamic from state of inaction to one of action, experimentation and willingness to try new things. Learn what these roles mean. Interview people you believe have these characteristics. Explore different opportunities. Use social media to find groups, networks, events, free conferences, meetups, and other venues for interacting with people who are doing things differently. Get motivated and get involved!

"BEING A CONTRIBUTION" ACTIVITY

Contribution occurs first on an individual level. What are you contributing to life around you on a daily basis? This is tactical and requires quick responses.

Leadership at the level of contribution to family, community and society is challenging. This level will require more time and effort. It is a process.

It is where a person either "shows up" or watches and waits for someone else to do the difficult work of taking a stand or voicing a concern or opinion.

"MAKING A DIFFERENCE" ACTIVITY

Answer the following questions and examine any insights gained as a result:

What does a life of contribution mean to you?

What difference do you or can you make that would add value, create meaning and purpose for yourself and others?

What difference does your life make to the world?

When you die and pass from this life, what legacy will you leave behind?

Make notes on your Life Story Timeline and begin a concerted effort to incorporate your contributions to life, work, family, community and society.

Our history will dictate our future if we allow it.

- Jo Singel

"PREPARING FOR LEADERSHIP" ACTIVITY

A critical success factor in preparing for leadership in life is to reach back to the past and identify outmoded, outdated and irrelevant ideas, concepts, theories, philosophies or attitudes that don't fit the vision of who you want to be now and in the future. As all of the previous activities have suggested, this is a process that takes time and effort. If you have been diligent with half of the activities and noted your insight, goals, thoughts and reflections on your Life Story Timeline you are well on your way to doing and being more than you may have thought possible. No one is above the work and it is literally never finished no matter what an individual has achieved. As the rate of change and disruption increases, these are the activities that will keep you vital, engaged, productive and energetic.

Now, it's important to take a further step back and look more deeply at what it is you've been carrying around with you throughout your life and experiences. What is contained within the mental storage unit? No matter what your age, background or environment, you've been around long enough to accumulate some useless even harmful baggage. Every day the stored baggage gets filled with more obstructions to achieving your desires. It can clog your brain and will inhibit or block your awareness so that no new information can filter through to your consciousness.

You are the master of your life. It is time to clear out some of the baggage that has either been taught to you or that you acquired all on your own in an effort to get things done quickly and either with urgency or expediency. In order to gain a personal philosophy, a unique and individual identity and leadership presence, you will need to determine who and what you will be in this life. That is where the unpacking the baggage process becomes important. It isn't enough to chuck everything into the mental garbage pail but now it is urgent that it is examined thoughtfully and carefully for either hidden gems, forgotten treasures, unfulfilled dreams or other useful items. First, a few questions need to be addressed and answered. This can take some time.

> What do you stand for as a leader?

> What is important to you?

> What really matters above all else?

> What prices are you willing to pay in order to stand by your values?

Once complete, and your are satisfied, it is time to begin pulling all of the pieces together.

With a clear mind, your values identified, your learning goals for developing and building your leadership ability is set and in motion. You have a definition or framework for leadership, and you are practicing awareness and presence. These tools are necessary for continued mental, emotional, spiritual and physical preparation for your leadership journey.

Know that a leader is always in a state of preparedness.

Expect the unexpected but don't get caught up in anxiety, fear, mental paralysis or hesitation. Continue to move forward and stay in action.

Circumstances or the drift of life will always impact us. How we deal with those unavoidable situations can and will make a difference in our lives and those of others.

"DEFINING LEADERSHIP FOR YOURSELF" ACTIVITY

Now that the path has been cleared and the ground prepared, the work of forging a leadership identity is increasing in intensity and urgency. Don't waste time looking back now as that task is complete.

Let's move forward and create the future. You will continue to be asked to reflect and respond to questions. If you have done the deep work in the prior activities you will notice a difference in your responses. As a reminder, this is a process of identifying, exploring, discovering and applying insights and gradually turning them into new behaviors, actions, traits and personal characteristics. The difference here is that it is a gradual process, more time consuming and thoughtful. Lasting transformation is accomplished in this way and others will notice a discernible difference in how you are presencing yourself whether at work, home or community. It is a process that is time tested and works.

"FURTHER DEFINING LEADERSHIP" ACTIVITY

Think about a situation where you were disturbed by a condition or experience you may have had regarding another individual, an event that occurred or what you may be reading or hearing about in the news.

Are there any actions you can take right now that would help to alleviate the condition?

Are there resources you have at your disposal that might help to make a contribution to bring about a more beneficial outcome to the situation?

How can you benefit from the opportunity to make a contribution? Would your participation enhance your sense of self worth? Would you have the opportunity to practice what you have been reflecting upon?

What small steps can you take at this moment toward reaching beyond where you are right now with regard to leadership in life?

If you don't feel ready or motivated to take a step, what is preventing you from taking action at this point in time?

What needs to be addressed so that you can move forward? Examples of what a leader strives to learn as they forge their identity:

- Make effective and better decisions
- Solve problems creatively
- Take risks and act assertively
- Set goals and stick with them
- Develop and execute on a plan of action
- Resolve conflicts with compassion, understanding and integrity

- Build strong relationships with people who embody similar values and goals
- Listen effectively and be open to different points of view and perspectives

"BEING EFFECTIVE AS A LEADER" ACTIVITY

In what areas do you want to be more effective?

List them.

What actions will you take to develop those characteristics?

What resources will you need?

"GOAL-SETTING" ACTIVITY

Consider the following process as you work toward achieving your goals.

As an individual who aspires or desires to strengthen their leadership development, what changes may be necessary as you proceed on the journey?

Take time to consider creating an action plan based on the following:

What I want to change about myself is:

What I expect to achieve as a result is:

Resources I'll need are:

Resources I have available to me are:

How I'll fill the gap between what I have and what I need are:

My timeframe for change is:

Milestones to be reached are:

Five reasons I need the change are:

Evidence of the change will be (new attitudes, skills and behaviors):

The prices I am willing to pay to have the change are:

My commitment to the change is: (on a scale of one to five; five being the highest level of commitment).

"RESPONSIBILITY" ACTIVITY

Responsibility has always been an important word associated with leadership. It has acquired numerous interpretations and meanings over the years. It's important for you, as a leader, to understand for yourself what responsibility means to you. Does it mean self-sacrifice? Or are you inclined to think of it as a duty or obligation? Whatever your interpretation, your perspective will shift depending upon the lens you are using.

"ENGAGING OTHERS" ACTIVITY

Consider how an effective and successful leader in the new world of work would interpret responsibility.

Observe someone you admire who, in your estimation, is taking responsibility for a problem or situation.

> What would they be saying or doing that conveys how they feel about being a responsible leader?

> When you observe or work with an individual who you consider responsible, how does it make you feel?

> What reactions or emotions do you have as a result of being in this individual's presence?

> When was the last time you felt a sense of responsibility? Perhaps you always feel responsible and it comes naturally to you.

> Or, you may never have considered exactly what it means to you and how the very act of responsibility itself is a tool of leaders.

> Consider the consequences of not taking responsibility. How does that make you feel?

> When would you refuse responsibility?

> What if someone were to ask you to do something you thought was unethical or made you feel uncomfortable?

> What would you do then and how would you handle the situation?

How do your leadership values, principles, goals and activities incorporate the answers to some of these questions?

In your estimation, what is your definition of a leader who acts with responsibility?

"VALUES" ACTIVITY

As a leader, you will need to gain clarity on your value system. Once you have identified which of your beliefs are self-generated versus imposed by others you may find a gaping hole in what you think you know about yourself. This is to be expected and not cause for alarm. As has already been mentioned, you must be the decider and the chooser.

What values ring true for you as an individual? No one will be able to assist you in answering this question. You are totally alone on this part of your journey.

Earlier in this journey, we covered RULES and DECISION-MAKING. Review your responses and make connections and look for patterns in this examination of VALUES.

"HAVING VOICE" ACTIVITY

Leadership voice is an inner communication. It is a self-empowering stand the leader takes for their life. The stand may not be articulated but it is assumed and will silently assert itself in all actions. More often than not, it is an inner voice guiding the leader throughout their life. It is a voice that says,

"I am the leader of my life. My thoughts, actions, dreams and desires are in my own hands."

As a leader hones their values and consciously and mindfully makes them visible in word and deed, the world begins to respond with feedback. Situations continually arise and you may begin to feel you are being tested regarding these values. Sometimes people ask if values can change. I believe some values are core to an individual's character and some have more to do with their personality and circumstances in life.

A leader's core values are the unspoken strengths that people feel as they experience the leader. What and how the leader communicates is felt verbally and non-verbally, as presence, energy and some would say charisma. It is not to imply that charisma or chemistry is a critical or necessary component of leadership. Some people are naturally charismatic and some are not. Charisma is not leadership.

Leadership voice, although more elusive than charisma and difficult to define, is a necessary tool. Without it, there is little or no projected personal power. Leadership voices come from deep within the heart and soul. Whether a leader is acting with good or bad intentions, the voice will tell you what you want or need to know.

Examples of Leadership Voice:

I am the leader of my own life.

I value all life.

I know and am true to myself.

I have deep trust and faith in who I am and all that I can be as a result.

I do not walk alone. I am supported in achieving my desired place in life.

I am loved and have love of life.

"HAVING A VISION" ACTIVITY

The next task in forging leadership identity is creating a well-defined and clear vision for personal leadership. Earlier we began exploring vision and now, we will take it deeper.

What does vision mean in a real time world? Why is this important?

Vision arises out of intention and is fueled by the satisfaction of achieving what you desire. Knowing that you have the freedom to create but also the opportunity to realize your goal is an exhilarating experience.

Knowing what you desire and having a picture of what it would look like if you were to achieve it is a powerful motivator. It is also a powerful narrative and enlivens the leadership story as it evolves over time.

Everyone arrives at their personal vision in their own way.

Some formalize the process by creating a physical piece of evidence of their vision. They create collages, journals, paint pictures, write it in a declaration or statement, purchase a small icon representing their vision or have a strong mental image that they recall from time to time to spur them on when they need a jolt of energy.

Begin with the questions:

> What is my vision for being a person possessing leadership talent and ability?
>
> What is my vision for what I want to accomplish in life?
>
> What is my vision for the kind of contribution I want to make as a leader?

Include your personal leadership vision in your Life Story Timeline. Notice where along the Timeline of your life you had a personal vision and where you did not. If you can, recall if there were any differences in your state of mind at that time.

"IDENTIFYING GAPS" ACTIVITY

As in all goal-setting and planning processes, it's important to identify obstacles, circumstances and challenges that could prevent the implementation of your plans.

Reflect on the questions:

> What could get in the way of your achieving your vision?

> What gaps in learning, knowledge or other resources do you have that could slow down your progress?

> What could accelerate achieving your goals?

Incorporate the information and knowledge you've learned into a new plan of action. Record your plan on your Life Story Timeline.

I will achieve my vision by:

> BEING...

> DOING...

> CREATING....

I will close the gap between my vision and my current reality by:

> DOING MORE OF...

> LESS OF...

> CONTINUING...

"POWERFUL QUESTIONS" ACTIVITY

What would the world be like if every person - regardless of their position, status or economic condition - were to think of themselves as a leader?

How can you assist others to step onto the path of an individualized, unique presence in the world?

Rehearse how you would respond differently, do something differently or take a new approach to how you typically solve problems and meet challenges and opportunity.

Communicate your results in a meaningful way so that others can gain from your experience, ideas and creativity.

Learning is essential to growing and changing. Whether as an individual being in leadership or in a leadership authority role, a leader's task is to help others learn.

- Jo Singel

Leadership is a state of mind.

- Jo Singel

WRAP-UP:

At this point, you have created a **vision** for your own personal leadership. You have identified **obstacles** to achieving your desires. You have examined **assumptions, beliefs and attitudes** that might derail your progress. You've cleared out the **baggage** of past experiences and your history to make room for the future. Now you will take these **goals**, attitudes and desires into the world and create your own **inspiring messages of leadership.**

What you can count on: Being in leadership will place you in situations where your thinking will be put to the test. High levels of self-awareness are key. It is essential your messages are consistent, clear and congruent. Being in integrity and authentic will differentiate you.

Visions are rarely fulfilled as the complete result of our own actions and activities.The kind of leadership we are addressing invariably requires that we align, influence, persuade, or sell our ideas and enroll the commitment of others to a common consciousness. The type of leadership we have been espousing is one in which everyone walks away a better person for having participated in the fulfillment of goals, ideas and missions. A leader interacts and impacts others throughout the process of realizing the vision and goals. Your values will guide your decisions, communications and act as your conscience. Not everyone will agree with the leader's vision and gaining commitment is not without its obstacles and challenges.

Leadership is always involved in change of any kind. Whether that is the launch of a new technology, the start of a new company, the implementation of a school project, the initiation of a disruptive idea, what is required to achieve the desired results is change and new learning. Many individuals and traditional leaders do not take that into consideration. What you have as an outcome is coercion versus cooperation, command and control behaviors, and lack of commitment, motivation and accountability on the part of those who are needed to make the vision a reality. Otherwise, you would be back where you began, going full circle toward having what you already had versus creating something new and innovative from what was before. Stepping into the stream, influencing the flow, the direction or the rate of speed is a task that requires skill, planning, strategy and action. As a leader, you will be accelerating the rate of change creation by understanding the change process, how and why people change or resist the new approach, and tools for reducing the risk of failure while enhancing the opportunity for success. **The Chapters ahead will address all of those needs.**

LEARNING CONCEPTS TOOLS, STRATEGIES AND TIPS FOR RAPID CHANGE

A LEARNING STORY

Imagine that you have decided, after many years of procrastination, to learn the language of your ethnicity. You want to get closer to your roots and converse in the language of your ancestors. You research the available opportunities and decide to attend a language school. Eager, hesitant, curious and excited for having taken the courageous step of putting yourself into an uncomfortable and unfamiliar situation, you take the plunge. The first day of school arrives. New pens, laptop and notebooks fill your carry-all bag. The other students are as eager as you are. Everyone is introduced and you wait for the teacher to arrive.

Finally, the door in the front of the room opens and in comes a woman with disheveled hair, obviously pregnant with child and a tired and worn-out expression on her face. It's obvious the woman would much rather be anywhere else but this classroom. The Teacher plops her book bags on the desk and without much introduction proceeds to let the class know this will be a very difficult term. There will be several hours of homework every night. The class will only speak in the language they will be learning and the Teacher will only converse in a foreign tongue. It appeared from the very heavily accented English any language was going to be a challenge.

Your heart starts racing and you can't understand why that would be the case. You are an adult, not a child held hostage in this classroom. You can leave any time you wish. There isn't any parent asking you about your day at school, wanting to know what your test score was or what homework you needed to complete for the night. Yet you feel anxious and afraid. The fear is escalating and you feel trapped and alone. What is going to happen here? The class begins and quickly you discover that you will not be able to keep up the pace. Other students have at least some experience with foreign languages. And something you had not anticipated is that the students are very competitive. Getting the correct answer is very important to them.

A week passes and you have now spent four hours each night preparing the homework for the following day's class. As you sit in your chair waiting to be called upon, your hands perspire, your mouth becomes dry and you dread hearing the sound of your own voice. You can't read what is in front of you. You can't comprehend the Teacher's instructions and worst of all, she corrects you and demands that you pronounce the words correctly. There is no respite and the pace is relentless.

Finally, in humiliation, you begin to complain to your classmates. Some drop out in frustration and others sit proudly as they display their fluency.

To add further to your insulted pride, you are the only individual in the class who is related to the language being learned. You and the Teacher share a common bond and she is relentless. "Mercy" is not a word in the woman's vocabulary.

You decide you have had enough. You are having nightmares of school years past when you struggled to grasp a math or science concept and stuttered embarrassed answers to the Teachers as classmates giggled.

School days are over for you now and you vow to never try that experience again.

But the story need not end on a negative note. There is an opportunity to prevent humiliating experiences from occurring when in a learning environment.

To provide context for a valuable lesson learned based on this story, consider the following ideas and concepts regarding how people learn best.

HOW WE LEARN

LEARNING AND CHANGE

Without learning, there can be no change. Learning itself is a skill. It is seldom taught. Further still, many highly educated people don't know how to teach people how to learn.

By the very nature of being a leader, you will be required to adapt, change and require others to do the same. Adapting, growing and changing will never occur unless an individual or group learns. An active and focused process needs to be undertaken in order to advance beyond the current state of knowledge and experience to a new desired state.

This is an important concept to grasp.

The goal of learning is to acquire new knowledge and experience so as to adapt, disrupt, innovate and transform.

For example, we learn and change in order to do something in an improved way, or in a way that has never been done before. As a result we learn new skills, solve problems differently and stimulate new thinking.

Without the capacity to learn there is little or no change that will occur except for what happens as a matter of circumstance or the consequence of an external event. Without learning there is little chance of creating new opportunities or being able to take advantage of them when they occur. Learning allows for innovation. Learning is a proactive state of mind, awareness and consciousness.

Through learning we create.

Oftentimes people are unaware of how they learn in spite of years spent in traditional academic environments. Unfortunately, many children have grown to fear the learning process. Frequently, and throughout an individual's life, learning is conducted in atmospheres of intimidation, competition and demand. Learning routine tasks is very different from applying a process that begins with curiosity and includes critical thinking, problem-solving, risk-taking and decision-making. Machine learning, Virtual Reality, and many other technologies and methods are disrupting how we help people learn.

Being uncomfortable is a part of learning. Some people experience confusion and anxiety which causes them to avoid learning new things. Being an inspiring leader means we need to understand how some people may feel and their reaction to any kind of change. They feel they will not be able to perform well. They are satisfied with how things are and have no interest in risking what they know for something that is unknown.

That is where the inspiration and vision of an individual leader can make the difference.

If fear is an obstacle to learning, creating a compelling motivation to change is critical. There is a profound difference between learning in a safe, comfortable, supportive environment where individual differences and styles are respected than in a cold, sterile and uncaring atmosphere. Of course, learning on-demand, on-line and from podcasts, videos and other media provide quick sharing of information and knowledge. But it is the philosophy of this author that lasting learning requires an on-going conscious process of generating new learning from what was learned before. This is what we are addressing here.

As we grow into full maturity, the human being becomes more sensitive to failure and mistakes. Humiliation does not increase the ability to learn but only suppresses it. This is why it is important for an individual who aspires to be in leadership or is a leader to understand how adults learn and the optimal ways in which to conduct experiences that will create optimal conditions for individuals to evolve from their current state to a future desired state.

LEARNING HOW TO LEARN

How many times a day does this occur where Teacher and Student, Manager and Employee are in a struggle to teach or learn something new? Most of the time it isn't so easy to quit. Fear, intimidation, humiliation, shame and embarrassment ruined many a life. Children quit school, fail to graduate and refuse to undergo the degrading experience of not being able to learn.

If you see your role as inspiring others to be in leadership in their work and lives, learning how to learn and helping others learn is an important step toward creating an individual identity and a leadership presence that is unique and powerful. The other options are more command and control, coercion, intimidation and being dictatorial.

When a person who is in leadership in life can help others learn, the contribution to another's life is enormous. Every adult who has forgotten what it is like to be a child, who stumbled, struggled for one reason or another with homework or classroom assignment should take a class in a subject that would be a challenge. Experience is the best teacher. And having the experience freshly in mind will close the case on why it is vitally important to understand what learning means and what is involved to help create a safe and supportive environment in which there is the chance the individual will be able to learn something new or different from what they already know.

You don't need a college degree to learn simple, basic fundamentals about learning that can and will make an enormous difference in what individuals will be able to achieve as a result.

What else do you need to know about learning?

The best place to begin is with the self.

Start by identifying how you learn best. This can be effectively accomplished through practice and trial and error. First, you must understand what learning is and means, how people learn and what obstacles stand in the way of learning.

PRINCIPLES OF LEARNING

Requires shifting from the present state to a desired future state otherwise learning will not occur. There will only be the status quo or "what already is"

Involves inquiry into "how we or others" think about something

Measurable outcomes; otherwise, we will not have a benchmark for what has changed

Involves unlearning from one state of knowing something to another

Always involves refreezing into a different state from the current state

Has an objective otherwise we wouldn't know what to expect as a result of our efforts

If successful will always cause a shift in perception, perspective or behavior

WAYS WE LEARN

People learn by:

Experience - by doing; activities

Reflection - self-awareness

Observation - paying attention and listening

Clarification – understanding

Feedback from others

Reading and applying

Role-Models

Mentors and Coaches

Powerful questions that challenge current perception

Reflect upon how you learn best.

- What do you need to enhance your learning skills?
- What prevents you from learning?
- What is the optimum environment for you to learn?

Oftentimes people confuse learning with training and consider both words to be interchangeable. They are not.

Learning is an active process of raising a question or hypothesis, "what do I want to know about a topic?"; testing various responses through research or trial and error; taking action on the information and finally reflecting upon the outcome.

Reflection involves self-discovery and occurs in many ways. People learn differently and at their own pace based upon motivation, desire and need.

Helpful questions will guide the learner toward their own conclusions:

> Did I learn from the situation?
>
> What was gained as a result?
>
> What worked well or didn't work so well?
>
> How do I apply what I learned to similar situations or to gain further knowledge of my topic or subject?

If and when learning occurs, there will be a change in behavior, attitude and sometimes, beliefs.

On the other hand, training is structured and focused upon a definable outcome. Training situations provide context, resources, suggestions, approaches and ideas that can then be applied by the learner in everyday experiences.

In training situations, individuals engage in simulated experiences. Oftentimes, the learner will gain valuable insights into a given behavior and will consider the opportunity to make alterations or change a belief or assumption. Follow-up with coaching, mentoring, web-based tools and further guidance on the topic to be learned are necessary components of successful training. Ensuring success in these situations is often based on what occurs after the training event.

STRATEGIES FOR SUCCESSFUL LEARNING

Leaders should apply thoughtful consideration to the following questions whether applicable to self or others:

What will the learner see, hear and feel during the experience?

Are there attractive, informative, well-presented visuals that reflect what is to be learned in the session?

Motivational proverbs and inspiring visuals help

What is the physical environment communicating?

If it's dull, boring, dirty, and uncomfortable, a message is communicated that people won't be respected and the learning won't be taken seriously. People may not understand this on a conscious level but they will experience it on a subliminal one.

Does the physical space appear as though it had been prepared for the people in attendance?

Are there adequate resources available?

Are there articles, websites, and checklists available after the learning experience to reinforce what was presented?

Are they attractive, free of typos and in sufficient quantity?

How is the seating arrangement presented?

For highly interactive sessions, a circle is best.

In more self-reflective work, chairs facing forward are effective.

Is there proper ventilation, not too hot or too cold?

Does the facilitator or teacher's appearance reflect and convey professionalism in such a way as to create credibility and respect?

What materials have the attendees received prior to the session to prepare them for the experience?

How will successful learning be measured? By whose standards?

Do the learners have follow-up activities?

> Learning is a process that needs to be applied and is acquired over time. It doesn't happen overnight. People will not suddenly walk away changed no matter what the threat is or how persuasive the argument.

Did the learner create a personal goal for the learning and a way to measure progress?

What resources, in the form of coaches or mentors, will assist the individual's learning process?

Is there a follow-up meeting scheduled where individual stories can be shared, lessons learned are identified and encouragement can be received?

Authentic, caring and compassionate leaders understand and take the time. They apply the resources and are available for guidance and support as they and others learn what it is they need and want to do to accomplish the objective. This type of leadership is and will continue to be in short supply. As an aspiring leader, you may consider the opportunity to take an active role in supporting learning.

KNOWLEDGE IS DIFFERENT FROM INFORMATION

Oftentimes, people mistake information they gain as knowledge learned. Information and knowledge are not the same. Information is easy to acquire and changes rapidly. Information is cheap and comes fast. Knowledge is expensive and is acquired more slowly. Information has a short shelf life. Knowledge lasts longer and is more difficult to unlearn. That is why learning comes with a price tag.

You need to let go of what you know and allow for the new awareness to take hold in your experience. Until then, you may feel uncomfortable, confused, and desperate for answers. The longer you can stay open and questioning the better. A tolerance for ambiguity is essential. You will "live in the grey" while acquiring new knowledge.

Consider the consequences of closing the door too soon. Leadership has always been about living in a grey zone, not black or white. Either/or thinking will only serve to keep you trapped in old ways of being and doing. Both/and thinking considers the pros and cons of an argument or piece of knowledge. It takes discipline and focus to learn.

Some good learning practices include:

> Discover as much as possible about your learning goal.
>
> Identify what it is you want and need to learn.
>
> Be specific and create ways to measure your progress.
>
> Identify opportunities for learning how to achieve the goal.
>
> Determine through trial and error what it is you need and want to learn.

Ask what resources others have used to achieve their learning goals.

Specifically, where did they go to learn what they wanted and who are the best teachers?

What books, websites and/or other written materials were useful?

Identify challenges to achieving the goal.

What would hinder you from learning your topic? Is there some skill you would need?

How can you go about acquiring it? Can you barter with someone who is an expert on the topic and exchange your knowledge for theirs?

Create a situation where you can test your newly acquired skills.

Is there a situation where you can volunteer your time that would provide you with the necessary environment for learning and developing your skills in the area of focus?

Find trusted colleagues who will provide you with feedback and additional resources.

Test and measure your progress against the feedback you receive from others who were aware of where you began your learning journey.

Seek a coach or mentor you know and respect and who knows and respects you. This can be the most valuable source of feedback.

Identify ways to repay your coach or mentor for the time they have taken to provide you with valuable input regarding your learning goals. Perhaps they require an occasional technology fix or other situation where your skills can help them to achieve their goals.

Conduct an After Learning Review.

What was it that you started out to achieve?

Where are you now regarding the goal?

What is still missing?

What will you do to address the gaps?

Develop a plan for continuing the learning process. Identify who, what, where, when and how you will continue to work on your learning goals.

LEARNING TO HELP OTHERS LEARN

Rarely will anyone embrace the unknown in favor of the known even when it is in their best interests to do so. And this is understandable. Our habits, attitudes, beliefs, conventions, rules and traditions define who we are – they are our collective and individual identity – hard earned, comforting, and nearly unchangeable.

As we go through life, we become increasingly accustomed to a daily process of adjusting and reacting to our internal and external environments and events all in an effort to maintain our equilibrium. Otherwise we feel lost, afraid, abandoned and insecure. These are feelings and emotions that we will do anything to avoid. They tie us up in knots of uncertainty and confusion and cause us to become paralyzed and unable to move in any direction.

Consequently, when we are asked to change, our very identity is being called into question. We may feel that we are being judged or wrong and that everything we've ever known, counted on, or been valued for will be lost. Then who will we be, what will we do, how will we survive in a world that is so vast and so confusing? Who we are is intricately tied up in what we do and have. Change will alter all that is known, tried and tested through hard-earned life experience.

Why would there be a need to change what has worked so well until now?

Your task as a leader is to present a vision that is powerful, compelling, understanding, clear and that will outlive the benefits, risks and rewards of changing **or** not changing.

The case for change must be seriously examined and reflected upon for flaws, personal biases, and perceived realities.

Change for the sake of change is not a reason to change. But change is constant and you, as a leader, will need to demonstrate that being ahead of the change is far less threatening than being at the effect of the change that is imposed from someplace outside of yourself.

HOW TO SHARE YOUR LEADERSHIP STORY TO HELP OTHERS LEARN

The leader's personal Life Story Timeline is a powerful tool that can be used to engage others in committing to a vision. The elements are your vision, mission, goals and a value proposition. Consider carefully what it is you share about yourself and how you frame your life's experiences, goals and desires to communicate what it is you want to achieve.

Reflect upon these questions:

What is the story of my life?

What were the challenges I faced early in my childhood?

How did I overcome them?

Who helped me?

Who hindered me and why?

What did I learn from these experiences?

What do I want to start, stop, and continue doing that will enable me to approach life fully confident that I have the capacity, the intelligence and the wherewithal to engage life as fully as possible?

Write a script that tells your story.

Two or three pages of typed material are sufficient.

Put a title on the top of the sheet, sign and date the document.

You are now on your way to creating your biography, which is different from your resume.

Your biography is your story, in your words, which communicates your journey. It could include your background and where or how you grew up, your earlier aspirations and what you've done to overcome obstacles, how you create opportunities for yourself and what you are passionate, curious and enthusiastic about achieving in your life.

This is your interpretation of your Life Story Timeline.

You don't need to share this story at this point, but in the future, you will use this story to create your compelling message of leadership as you assist and support others toward changing, learning and growing into their leadership vision.

Notice how leaders in positions of authority always communicate details of their lives as they illustrate a point, request your commitment, and influence your perceptions of who you think they are.

Leaders tell stories. As a leader, you have a story to share with others to inspire and create your leadership presence.

Write your story and file it in your leadership portfolio for future review.

"PEERS ASSISTING OTHER PEERS" ACTIVITY

CONSIDER WHO YOU CAN LEARN FROM. WHO DID THIS BEFORE?

If you:

Want to learn about a new topic

Have few resources

Want to learn from others mistakes and experiences

Do the following:

1. Identify three or four people SMEs (Subject Matter Experts) who have been successful in your field of endeavor.
2. Clarify what it is you are intending to accomplish.
3. You will gain more respect for your request if you can effectively articulate your goal. SMEs are not there to help you figure out what it is you want. That is your job.
4. If you don't know any SME's, ask people in your social network if they can tap into their network for you.
5. Assess who you want to contact based on your topic.
6. You don't need to communicate with everyone. Choose carefully. Time is a valuable resource.
7. Prepare a list of questions.
8. Write a script. Identify who you are, what you want, and who referred you.

You can:

Place a call or send an email introducing yourself, your contact if necessary and your request. Ask for assistance and not advice.

Acknowledge the individual's area of expertise that you want to tap.

WHAT'S THE MOTIVATION FOR THE SME? WHAT DO THEY GET OUT OF IT AND HOW DO YOU "SELL" THEM ON IT?

Schedule a thirty to forty-five minute meeting in a location that is convenient for the SME.

A phone conversation is sufficient. Most of the time, face-to-face meetings are difficult to schedule, especially if this individual is an expert in their field.

Begin with an open-ended question to warm up and begin the conversation.

Consider including the following questions:

How did you go about learning your subject?

(This is similar to looking at the bibliography of a book or a research paper. It will provide you with more leads as you seek the knowledge you need.)

Who was most influential for you?

(Determine the SMEs belief system about your topic. You may or may not agree with their conclusions.)

What was your greatest lesson learned?

Determine if the SME is using someone else's knowledge or if it was based on their own hard-earned experience.

What, if anything, would you do differently if you had to go about it today?

(How reflective is your SME? How up-to-date is their thinking on the topic?)

What would you continue doing if you had to do it all over again?

(Again, determine how reflective the SME is and how valid their knowledge is concerning your topic.)

How did the experience change your perspective?

(Is the SME thinking more broadly or more narrow in scope?)

If you were me, who should I talk with next or use as a resource?

(It doesn't hurt to tap their resource pool.)

IN CONCLUSION

Thank the SME for their time and send a thank you note either on personalized note paper or via email.

Acknowledge their assistance and openness to sharing their knowledge and wisdom in a thoughtful and carefully crafted note.

Once you've gathered your data begin the process of assessing what is relevant to your project.

Discard anything that isn't adding value. Remain focused on what it is you desire to accomplish right now.

While you are in the middle of learning and implementing, it's important for you to check in from time to time with a few of your SME's to determine whether or not you are:

> Heading in the right direction

> Have the appropriate information

> Are not acting on previous assumptions that may not be relevant to your task

It's important to take into consideration that you may have tried something similar and experienced failure. As a result, you may carry over certain biases, feelings or emotions into the situation.

What you may not realize is that those very same biases may have contributed to your failure. Ensure you aren't on the path to creating a self-fulfilling prophecy.

LEARNING AS A COMMUNITY EFFORT

IDENTIFY WHO ELSE WANTS TO LEARN THE TOPIC

Find someone else who is trying to learn the same things that you are and trade experiences.

CREATE A SMALL COMMUNITY OF LEARNERS

Consider forming a learning team or buddy group. Create a schedule to meet, talk on the phone or exchange emails so that you can motivate each other to achieve small, achievable goals.

SHARE RESOURCES WITH OTHERS INTERESTED IN LEARNING

Exchange books and other relevant resources such as websites, networking groups and associations with one another or create an online chat room and use a simple technology tool to store the information online.

BE A LEADER

These things rarely work without some type of leadership.

Here is an opportunity to be in leadership regarding the subject you want to learn.

BE AN EXPERT. BE KNOWN FOR SOMETHING. BE A RESOURCE

It is also an opportunity to become a subject matter expert. Once you have successfully implemented your goal, people will begin to call on you for support and resources.

Be available for others. Keep the knowledge and wisdom flowing and you will be rewarded when others share with you.

LEARNING FROM THE LESSONS OF OTHERS ACTIVITY

What works well when "learning from others"?

BENEFITS

People generally report:

- It was relevant to something I was trying to complete at the time.
- The person took the time to answer my questions.
- I had time to practice.
- I wasn't frightened of being humiliated but felt relaxed and calm
- Everyone was in the same situation as me. I wasn't the only person trying to do this.

Conduct a web search to determine what resources are available that could help jumpstart your learning journey, including communities with similar interests and passions.

Keep a daily or weekly journal or diary to document your thoughts, feelings, concerns and challenges.

"IDENTIFY WHAT YOU NEED TO LEARN" ACTIVITY

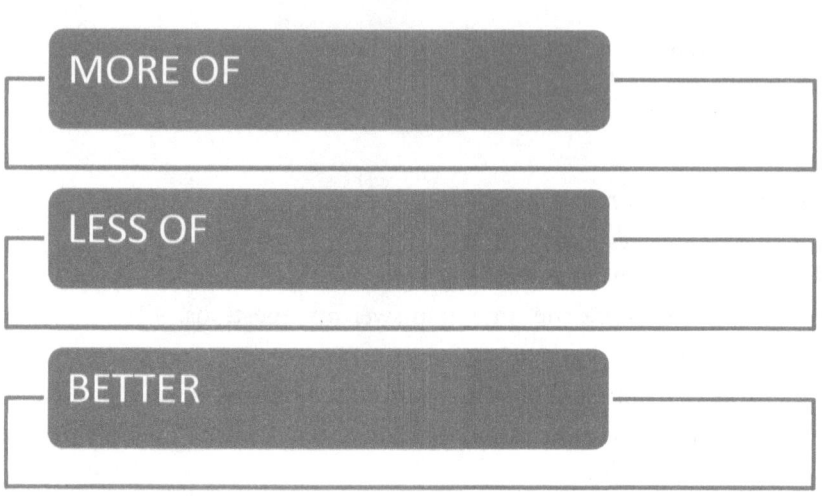

MORE OF

LESS OF

BETTER

You may discover some things that are outside of the goal and timeframe you created for achievement.

In order to stay on track, but not lose the data, indicate in your framework what's relevant to your goal and what isn't.

HOW TO HELP GROUPS BE BETTER COLLABORATORS ACTIVITY

Setting up meaningful group learning activities can be a great boon to enabling change in any environment.

There are numerous benefits of group learning activities if there is an intention to grow and develop the individual members. The benefits are numerous. Members will:

> Gain wisdom and perspective that is different than their own

> Develop tolerance and respect for diversity of opinion

> Develop tolerance for failure as a necessary ingredient when an outcome is not assured and the path taken is new and relatively untested. So long as failure is not the end game, you aren't experiencing anything different from anyone else. The important thing is to learn from the failure.

> Foster longer-term thinking

GUIDELINES

Establish a few Guiding Principles for meetings:

> Agree to build a trusted, reliable, committed, passionate and curious group of individuals who have a common aspiration of achieving goals, sharing knowledge and information.

Build the group with individuals who believe that together they are more powerful than acting alone in their learning experience.

Articulate the values that the group holds as contributing to each member and to the group.

Create ground rules for the norms and rules – what is acceptable and non-acceptable behavior during meetings and for specific tasks.

HOW TO HELP TEAMS LEARN

This is an activity which, when conducted over time, can increase the value of your results because of the accumulated experiences and knowledge you've gained as you apply what worked and what didn't work to the next activity. Your ability to learn will increase and you will make fewer and fewer mistakes.

The activity works with individuals as well as groups and teams of people who have been working on an activity or a project together. It's important to determine what it was that you intended to achieve as a result of the activity.

Ask:

What was supposed to happen as a result of my efforts?

What actually happened when I took action?

What happened to cause the difference between what I intended and what resulted?

What should I do differently the next time so that I get closer to the result I want to achieve?

What could have gone better?

If you are conducting this activity for yourself, allow 15 minutes and document the results.

For teams, allow for 30 minutes and ensure that everyone understands the implications of the discussion.

THE CHANGE PROCESS FRAMEWORK

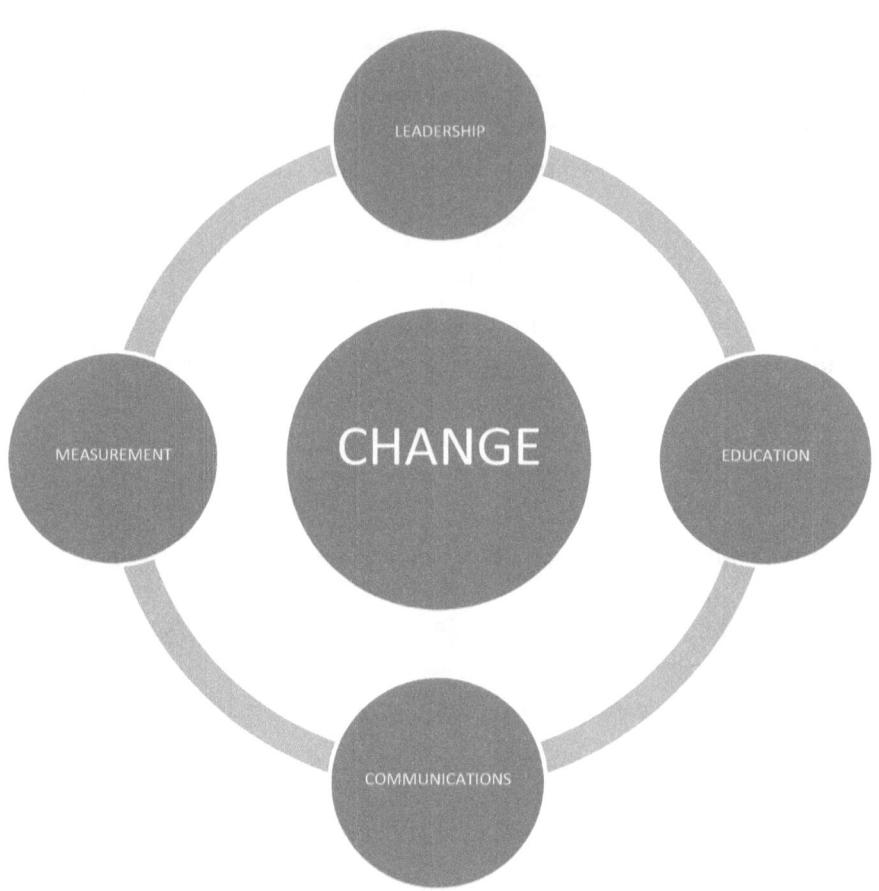

THE HUMAN SIDE OF CHANGE

As most people are aware, change is a constant. A key leadership skill is the ability to change, adapt and grow. But in order to change, a leader must possess the ability to learn.

Without learning, there is no change. Nearly all change requires new skill-sets, behaviors or attitudes. Learning itself is a skill and is seldom explained or taught. Further still, many highly educated people lack the knowledge of how to teach people how to learn.

Many a business, families and communities have failed to grow and enrich the lives of its members because they were unable to learn, change and grow together. They didn't know how to learn together so that their vision, goals and values could withstand the inevitable process of change. Decay and disillusionment resulted rather than renewal and transformation into a more viable and vibrant business or community.

Their communities were no longer sustainable.

An example that most people can relate to is a convenience store they must frequently use or visit. Time after time, the same mistakes are made by mindless and repetitive actions that result in the same outcomes. You get the feeling that everyone is bored or uninterested.

Imagine this scenario played out in the numerous institutions, organizations and bureaucracies you must frequent in order to live in your community. It is rare that the average person doesn't, at least once a day, shake their heads in amazement at all of the nonsensical things they witness every day.

We are all guilty of ignorance. Sometimes the act of learning can feel like an uphill battle. Of all the attributes that differentiate effective from ineffective action, learning is a key contributor to success or failure.

Most of the time people are performing their tasks without benefit of reflection or taking a step back to identify, examine and analyze what has worked and why and what hasn't worked and why not.

Learning and possessing the know how to teach others to learn are key leadership attributes. It is the only way the leader will be able to sustain any gains they may have achieved through their best efforts.

"HOW TO PREPARE PEOPLE FOR CHANGE" ACTIVITY

People need information and knowledge with regard to the change they are implementing. Otherwise they will be confused, paralyzed and unable to move forward.

For people who are acting from your leadership or guidance it will be essential to do the following:

1. Understand the risks and rewards of the change and communicate them clearly in compelling messages.
2. Commit to an energizing and engaging vision of change. Your own enthusiasm and excitement will inspire people to get on board with the change.
3. Paint a picture of the vision for change that others can understand.

Be patient and tolerant of others ability to learn and grow with the change. They will not have the benefit of knowing precisely what your vision is unless you continually communicate your ideas and plans and engage them in a dialogue, which is inclusive, empowering, caring and compassionate.

A leader must pay careful attention to the following:

> Clearly identify what it is that you expect. Carefully explain what the individual's role is in the change process.

> Identify the expectations of yourself and others. Be realistic and continue to guard against overreach, self-fulfilling prophecies, and making assumptions about your environment.

> Understand what the boundaries are between the commitment of others and your own determination to implement the goal.

Provide support in helping your stakeholders deal with the natural resistance to change including fear and discomfort of having to learn something new.

Provide a safe environment for learning while understanding that no one likes to look bad, be wrong or humiliate themselves in front of others.

Remember that learning takes time and big change won't happen quickly.

Identify ways to measure progress.

Celebrate successes along the way.

Don't withhold praise for fear that people will get comfortable. Understand that way of thinking is a myth learned from others who only knew one way to create and manage change.

Remember that all learning involves change. No learning, no change. It is only burdensome when the leader is in reactive mode, always putting out brush fires and never planning for the inevitability of having to deal with challenges.

HANDLING SELF-FULFILLING PROPHECIES

Self-fulfilling prophecies can make or break the execution of any vision and sabotage any change.

WHAT IS A SELF-FULFILLING PROPHECY?

Human beings are in a constant state of judging, forming opinions, making generalizations and pre-assessing situations. This is normal.

Survival instincts and our hard-wiring predispose us to think ahead of our opponents, consider who or what may threaten our existence or how to conserve energy, resources and will-power.

It is not the fault of the human character but how it is that we are still standing after a few thousand years of existence.

Once again, the tools and resources that enhance the human being's survival rate were appropriate in an age when life held many physical threats such as encountering a hungry tiger, poisonous snake or other enemy.

That was the past.

In today's world, prejudging a situation without testing assumptions can threaten a successful outcome just as harshly as a surprised bear could remove one of your limbs.

Authentic leadership holds you to a higher standard and requires that you transcend the basic essentials of survival.

Relying on instinct or intuition will help to sustain life at a survival level but those tools alone will not support growth and development beyond the cave stage.

A self-fulfilling prophecy is:

> A predetermined set of beliefs and conclusions applied to a person or group.

> It predicts their actions and behavior based upon your own point of view and perspective.

> It is not based on experience with the individual or group or any previous behavior or actions.

> It can simply be your perspective or perceived reality.

> It is untested and generally you will be tempted to search for evidence to prove that your assumptions were correct.

Why do self-fulfilling prophecies harm or sabotage our efforts?

Oftentimes, people make generalizations and conclusions that are false.

False information does not support success and will ensure failure. Many times, this behavior will encourage people to cover up the information and to hide false assumptions that created havoc.

People don't like to be wrong and will do anything to avoid looking bad.

What can a leader do to avoid making self-fulfilling prophecies?

Leaders can:

Understand that making assumptions and pre-judging is normal and that no one likes to be wrong, taken by surprise or not have the answers.

Take time and apply resources toward testing assumptions, beliefs, prejudices, judgments, and perceptions about the situation and people involved.

The process takes time and energy.

Do you want to disrupt or change "what is"? If not, then test your assumptions so they don't become self-fulfilling prophecies.

Think about some self-fulfilling prophecies you've experienced lately. How did it turn out for you and others?

HANDLING ASSUMPTIONS ACTIVITY

As you create and share your plan for taking new actions toward achieving your strategic goals, you will encounter individuals who may or may not be supportive of your aspirations.

SHOULD YOU BE CONCERNED?

Yes.

Most goals require cooperation, assistance, support and the actions of others, especially if you are committed to being in leadership in life.

It is important for you to identify and pre-determine the individuals you will engage as you take action in your environment. These individuals are called your "key stakeholders" which include influential individuals, potential investors, talented resources, advisors, board members, partners and collaborators.

WHERE TO START

Begin by reviewing your goals and identifying who has a stake in helping you achieve them.

Make 3 lists:

A. Anyone who will be involved in decision-making
B. People who are influential in your field – their sphere of influence is greater than your own
C. People who have specialized expertise, skills and competencies who can act as Advisors, Board Members and other predetermined roles

Once you have determined the individuals, assess their stake using the following questions.

What does each individual have to gain or lose as a result of the intended outcome?

What will motivate them to agree or disagree with what it is you want to achieve?

How do you think they will resist or what objections might they have about your idea or proposed change?

What might they do to thwart/help your efforts?

How might they sabotage your efforts through intentional negative press or use of social media?

Who will be supportive of your success and who might be an ally?

Now, test your assumptions.

How do you know that the assumptions you made are true about the individuals you analyzed?

What evidence is there that any of the answers to the questions are truth and reality?

How did you arrive at believing these answers to be true? What specifically did the individuals involved do or say to cause you to believe they would react in the same way?

What do you need to do differently to test your assumptions about your key stakeholders?

WHY IS THIS A CRITICAL TASK?

What you are identifying is the rate or amount of resistance you think or feel the stakeholders will have with regard to the change you want to create.

It is important for a leader to understand the concept of natural occurring **human resistance to change** in a way that empowers the goal rather than challenges the effort.

Evaluating pre-determined assumptions can make the difference between success or failure of any change effort or new venture.

"RESISTANCE TO CHANGE" ACTIVITY

Resistance to change is natural. When there is no resistance, the leader should be alert to the possibility that there may be someone or something that will arise which will attempt to sabotage or place the change in jeopardy.

DOING PULSE CHECKS

Find ways to communicate about the change, which arouses reaction so you can understand the motivation behind resistance.

Pay careful attention to non-verbal behaviors. Don't become paranoid. Use a reasonable amount of skepticism, accepting the fact that resistance to change is a normal human condition. Even people who claim to love change will have a reaction to a new idea. Their way of resisting the new idea is to question, "tear it apart", try to find reasons "why it won't work" or similar behaviors. Some hide the feeling of "resistance" behind the word "feedback".

Create communications activities, which allow for both public disclosure as well as anonymous input.

Check in with individuals who typically have a finger on the pulse of the communities in which you are involved and who matter to your efforts.

Graciously accept all feedback and **reward versus punish** people for their honesty.

Don't attempt to persuade people they are "wrong" or "don't understand".

Continue to work the process; reinforce key messages; continue testing and experimenting. Focus on **educating and communicating.**

Sometimes you will just have to go with your gut; go out on a limb and do what you need to do regardless of resistance, skepticism or negativity.

There are numerous examples of change agents, entrepreneurs and leaders who have gone against the grain and were enormously successful.

MORE TIPS TO CONSIDER

Don't assume that when people are quiet that they are on board with what it is that you want to create.

Remember that you are asking people and yourself to change. How will you resist your own plan for change? Prepare for it.

People need to be right and look good. Change will cause people to have to learn new skills, concepts, and ways of behaving or believing. There is fear that they will be wrong or fail. Ensure people are safe and have sufficient communication, education and knowledge so they can succeed. Self-confidence and self-esteem will be enhanced and engagement will be higher as a result.

Oftentimes leaders react with anger and hostility when they encounter resistance which only further drives resistance deeper while creating a nearly insurmountable wall. In this scenario, no one wins.

YOU CAN'T COMMUNICATE ENOUGH

Communicate all the ways that are available to learn that minimize the risk of failure, support, accountability, attention to detail and commitment.

Walk the talk.

Learn alongside of others.

Demonstrate what is new.

Ask for feedback.

Be honest.

CHECKING ASSUMPTIONS

Nothing endangers change and learning more than placing judgments on people and situations without checking the assumptions upon which the "truth" was based. What we think about most has a way of controlling our own actions and behaviors and creating the results we fear most.

Self-reflect

Frequently request feedback

THE HUMAN CONDITION

The need to be right all of the time, to look good and be in absolute control are among a leader's deadliest enemies during times of change.

THAT MAY SOUND LIKE A SHOCKING STATEMENT.

It is not. These enemies live within the leader's own psyche and must be dealt with on a daily basis. They tend to kill feedback and criticism, setting people up to fail, and create a wall of defensiveness that cannot be penetrated. New knowledge cannot enter the wall built by these enemies. New learning cannot occur, as the mind is too busy defending what it already knows how to do well. Past success can become a breeding ground for future failure.

Many of the leaders WE DO NOT ADMIRE fall into this very human trap.

They show up as:

Command and Control bosses

Micromanagers

Paranoid Dictators

If you are fearful of becoming this type of Leader, you will need to be MINDFUL of the human condition and what lurks inside of you.

Stay aware and self-conscious.

Be honest with yourself.

Acknowledge where you need to be resilient, adaptive, open and as non-judging as possible.

Everyone judges. What makes the difference is how much and with what frequency we judge both ourselves and others.

TIPS IMPORTANT ENOUGH TO REPEAT

HOW TO MANAGE RESISTANCE TO CHANGE

Accept that resistance is a natural reaction to change.

Empathize with your stakeholders, audience or individuals who will be affected by your change.

Identify your stakeholders concerns by asking open-ended questions. Don't attempt to advocate or persuade for a particular position. Instead, inquire into what it is people are attracted to and may fear that they will lose as a result of this change.

Understand your own biases, opinions, beliefs and assumptions about the stakeholders, audience and individuals you are addressing with the change you want to create.

Identify what the "gain" or benefit is for each of your key stakeholders. Every individual or group has its own stake in the change – what's in it for them?

Have the courage to hear people's concerns without fear that once heard or acknowledged the responses will become reasons for not changing. Hold yourself accountable to a higher standard of behaving.

Know what the "comfort zone" is for people involved in the change and what the risks are that they will need to incur in order to move forward in the direction of the change.

Identify and acknowledge the price you are willing to pay to have the change occur. Understand the prices others are paying in terms of time, energy and fear of ego-damaging failure.

It is natural for people to desire to preserve and protect their own way of doing things even if those behaviors, attitudes and activities maintain a status quo that is no longer viable.

Oftentimes, people will not want to expose what they feel is their ignorance and will shy away from talking with a potential role model or mentor. That is why it is important to feel the tension between what you want and where you are now – keeping your vision or goal in clear line of sight. It will help to get you over your natural fears and concerns and allow you to pay the price to achieve your dreams. The more you do to keep the payoff in sight, the greater your motivation will be.

ATTENDING TO THE EMOTIONAL SIDE OF CHANGE

As a leader, you know the importance of having a powerful set of tools to empower and assist others in learning, growing and evolving. The following is a set of guidelines for acknowledge and tending to the emotional side of change.

1. Help people find personal meaning and value in what is being requested of them.
2. Allow for time, care and a positive intention to take the place of platitudes, slogans and mantra.
3. Pay attention to your language – it needs to be in integrity with how and what it is that you are requesting. Sometimes the leader must find a new language, one they may not be familiar with or comfortable using. But if the change is to create a different world, a different language is necessary to explain what the new vision is.
4. Respect that people change at different rates and not everyone will immediately jump on board and embrace a new vision.
5. Create meaningful, measurable steps so that everyone knows how well the change is progressing and where the roadblocks are.
6. Listen carefully to feedback and respect what is heard; translate the feedback into meaningful actions and new behaviors.

Work on a plan to address these guidelines. Continue to incorporate new information and knowledge as you forge your leadership identity, develop your vision, take new actions and practice new behaviors.

TEAMS LEARNING TOGETHER FOR RAPID CHANGE

"TEAMS FORMATION AND PERFORMANCE" ACTIVITY

First, they strive to get to know one another and assess strengths, weaknesses, level of commitment to goals and willingness to do the work.

Second, they oftentimes get to the point where they disagree and/or engage in conflict.

Third, with a healthy team, they will settle down into a normal routine of work and engaging with one another.

Finally, they get to the point where goals are being achieved.

"HIGH-FUNCTIONING TEAMWORK" ACTIVITY

During the early formation of a team, it's important for the leader, change agent or individuals who take up a leadership role to help the group to work with:

A clear set of goals

Ground rules for how they will work together

An understanding of what the task is to be accomplished

WHY IS THIS IMPORTANT?

In a surprising number of cases, unclear goals, lack of a mindful process of how best to work together and unfamiliarity with the information being addressed is a norm. This is the case whether it is a graduate school project, business initiative or entrepreneurial venture.

If the groundwork is not carefully laid at the beginning of the project or collaboration, a team can flounder for a long time in endless debate over who is right and who is wrong. Oftentimes, individual team members will have differing opinions of what the actual goal is and how to go about achieving it. Keeping in mind the following points can be helpful.

People have different styles that include:

Conflict Resolution

Decision-Making

Problem-Solving

Learning

Managing Time and Prioritizing

Organization

Planning

Oftentimes people don't realize these styles are actual skill-sets as well and fall under the category of "management".

Management has come to be known as a ROLE rather than a set of skills to organize, plan, evaluate, analyze and a host of other competencies necessary for implementing goals, missions and simply getting a product or service to market.

Everything we do to achieve goals involves these management skills and competencies.

Management is a process of DOING
versus
Leadership is a way of BEING.

Mix in personality characteristics, brain wiring and simple preferences. You can easily see why it is challenging to accomplish goals in highly complex, ever-changing environments.

Technology creates efficiencies of scale.

Human beings must still manage and lead efforts, decide which tools make the most sense and help themselves and others learn new methods on a continuous basis.

Spending an appropriate amount of time upfront will create considerably better outcomes for all involved.

"TEAMWORK" ACTIVITY

1. A team should reflect upon and formulate responses to the following questions:

    What are we here to do?

2. Set a specific amount of time to answer this question before moving on to the next set of questions.

    How shall we organize ourselves?

    Who is the leader or facilitator?

    Who cares about our success? Our failure?

    How do we work through our problems?

    What challenges might we face? How should we handle them?

    How do we fit with other groups?

    What benefits do team members need from the team?

"HOW TO FACILITATE EFFECTIVE GROUP CONVERSATION" ACTIVITY

DO'S AND DON'TS

Pay attention to the bigger picture perspective; help others do the same.

Refrain from taking a position early on; it will squelch honesty and fair debate of the issues.

Rephrase what you think you heard; explore others thought process with honesty, objectivity and consistency.

Refrain from disregarding your own feelings, values and insights.

See if you can arrive at conclusions that move beyond validating your own position.

Examine your assumptions that led to the current reality.

Allow your opinions to be influenced by others – encourage your assumptions to be challenged by others.

Practice self-disclosure – how you arrived at a position, what led to the thinking and how it may have affected others.

Examine where you may have taken a defensive position and ask yourself:

What was the situation? Reflect upon what happened as a result.

How did you behave under the circumstances that were occurring?

Were you pleased with the outcome?

If you weren't satisfied, what might you have said or done differently to realize a different outcome?

How would that have affected the result of the discussion?

What can you take away from the experience that would benefit you in the future?

"HOW TO CONDUCT AN EFFECTIVE MEETING" ACTIVITY

1. Assign an individual to be the timekeeper; establish a system of rotation so that everyone has an opportunity and responsibility for keeping the momentum going.
2. Identify a few goals that can be accomplished within a reasonable timeframe.
3. Conduct individual audits that represent the collective knowledge and wisdom of the network.
4. Identify gaps – where the network needs additional resources or other stakeholders who can be tapped for specific knowledge and information.
5. Establish a system where documents will be stored and shared.
6. Have a clear intention that everyone knows and understands, allowing for individual visions.
7. Determine whether or not it makes sense to develop a network project that members can use as a pilot or proto-type for future learning together.

Facilitate a "question and answer" period to determine what worked well and what didn't work during the meeting; incorporate what was learned in the next meeting and in your guiding principles.

"HOW TO EVALUATE EFFECTIVE TEAMWORK" ACTIVITY

This activity can be used after team meetings to help the individual members reflect on what took place during the time spent on a particular topic.

As a leader, you are promoting the idea of reflection that leads to learning. You can use the tool to establish a context for a conversation that holds everyone accountable and responsible for creating results.

Too often, individuals will talk about how ineffective a meeting was after the fact rather than at a time when action can be taken to course-correct.

Applying after action reviews signals the team that participation in meetings is key and their performance will be rewarded according to the quality of their input and ideas.

Complete the following statements:

1. My participation as a team member so far has been:
2. The degree to which my ideas have been listened to by other team members is:
3. The degree to which the team is really working together is:
4. My satisfaction with my membership in this team is:
5. Based on our level of teamwork today, I predict the rating of our teamwork two months from now will be:

"HOW TO CONDUCT A TEAM MEETING DEBRIEF" ACTIVITY

This tool can be used to assist a team in conducting further evaluation of their planning process. It is essential to have an activity in place which supports the behavior of adjusting, improving and course-correcting your mission or goal achievement.

What's working/what's not working?

What should we do more of? What should we discontinue doing?

How effective have our strategies been to date?

Are our strategies helping us attain the desired results?

Are we gaining ground on the result or are we coasting in place?

What will move us closer to the results?

What happens to us when things don't go as we expected?

Do we re-group, discuss and take an honest account of what we have been doing?

Or, do we continue on the same path, hoping for a breakthrough?

How do we typically handle obstacles? Do our attitudes and behaviors help or hinder us?

Are there any team members who are not pulling their weight?

How do we address these sensitive issues?

Who can help us facilitate a process to handle upsets the team may be experiencing?

How do we handle the time gap between actions and results?

What are our constraints?

How do we feel about the leadership of the team?

What changes do we need to make in order to ensure our success?

TOOLS FOR
LEADER- MENTORS

LEADERS AS MENTORS OF CHANGE

A powerful change tool is mentorship. One-on-one assistance to customize a learning/action plan for individual development is one of the surest ways to enable success during change or help someone through a steep learning curve.

Leaders engage in mentoring others as they learn and grow.

It is an important resource and critical tool for leaders to learn and to teach others how to mentor and coach their protégés.

The following guidelines are designed for mentees to use as you take a proactive approach to learning what it is you need to learn on your leadership journey. An individual aspiring to be a leader in life finds out what is needed and creates approaches to achieve their goals.

> Don't wait for someone else to take the initiative to reach out and invite you to be coached.

> Take charge and determine who or what it is that can provide you with an opportunity to accelerate your ability to learn.

> Given that learning takes time and time is a resource that is in increasingly short supply, you will need to use effective tools to help you in the process of learning.

A leader can share an enormous amount of knowledge in the form of tips, strategies and guidelines for those undertaking or undergoing change.

TOOLS FOR LEADING RAPID CHANGE

HOW TO MAKE MEETINGS PRODUCTIVE

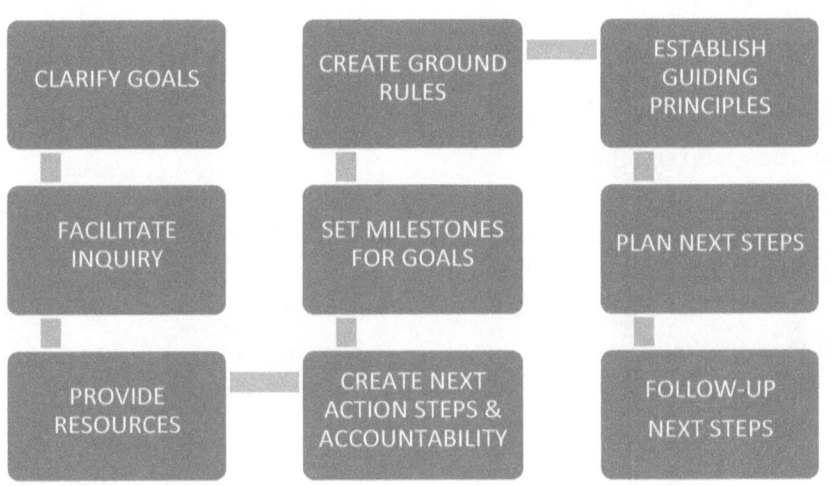

GROUND RULES FOR EFFECTIVE MEETINGS

If you are leading a meeting or developing the agenda for one, use these ground rules to quickly initiate a dialogue with the team about the most effective methods to create a successful outcome for your meeting regardless of the group size.

Establish and agree upon a set of ground rules that will go a long way toward creating a successful outcome.

It isn't always comfortable to suggest a structured approach to meetings. But there are meetings between individuals or groups where the stakes are high enough to risk any push back to the idea.

Professional groups hire mediators, negotiators and facilitators. You may not always have the luxury of time or expense to undertake the hiring of such an individual. The more equipped you are to handle all contingencies the better. The more knowledgeable you are regarding the proper set up, structure and dynamics of an effective meeting, the better you will be able to judge the effectiveness of an individual who makes their living providing these services.

Pay attention to the bigger picture perspective

Refrain from taking a position early on

Rephrase what you think you heard

Explore with honesty, objectivity and consistency

Refrain from disregarding your own feelings, values and insights

See if you can arrive at conclusions that move beyond validating your own position

Examine the assumptions that lead to a current position

Establish a place to maintain and share documents relative to the needs of the network

Have a clear intention that everyone knows and understands, allowing for individual visions

Determine whether or not it makes sense to develop a network project that members can use as a pilot or proto-type for future learning together

Conduct an after action review to determine what worked well and didn't work well during the meeting; incorporate the lessons learned in the next meeting and in the guiding principles

TIPS AND STRATEGIES
FOR RAPID CHANGE

PRACTICING NEW BEHAVIORS TAKES TIME AND ENERGY

Practice is important, especially if you are learning a new behavior for the first time. Knowing you may not achieve one hundred percent of your goal will help you set realistic expectations.

CELEBRATE SMALL WINS

It's important to celebrate small successes and reward yourself for your efforts.

DO TIMELY PULSE CHECKS

Stay in tune with emotions that you have during the first stage of learning something new. Oftentimes, people feel uncomfortable when learning something new. They may be reluctant to share their goals with others for fear of ridicule, criticism or judgment.

SELF-JUDGING CAN SABOTAGE EFFORTS

The voice of judgment can be very strong especially when conditioned by years of being told what your capabilities are or what others expect of you.

Don't allow other people to set limitations on you. They are only projecting their own fears and subconsciously will not want you to succeed, especially if it's something they tried to do and failed.

RELAX AND ENJOY THE JOURNEY

Be kind to yourself and know that everyone will learn at their own pace. Some individuals need to understand the context first or the big picture.

Others will focus on details requiring a need to maintain a high level of energy and positive mental framework to keep their vision in clear sight.

MAKE YOUR VISION VISIBLE

Creating a vision board with pictures of you achieving your goals is motivating and helps to create a very positive self-fulfilling prophecy.

LEADERSHIP LESSONS

There will always be lessons in life to learn. Here is a list of lessons we have learned about the kind of leaders we aspire to always be.

#1   Leaders live on purpose.

    #2   Leaders make choices based on a vision or goals they create for where they want to be and what it is they want to be doing.

#3   Leaders own who they be in the world. No excuses.

    #4   Leaders plan, do, think, course correct, pay attention to what they and others are feeling, how they are impacting those around them including their communities and environment.

#5   Leaders identify and live their values.

    #6   Leaders initiate, take stands and risk not looking good, not being right, not always being in control.

#7   Leaders pay a price for what they believe in.

    #8   **Leaders never rest on their laurels or take being a leader for granted. They are always in a state of learning, evolving, changing and growing.**

WHAT DID YOU WANT AND NEED TO LEARN?

WHAT DO YOU NEED TO DO NEXT?

LEARNING

WHAT ACTUALLY HAPPENED?

WHERE WERE THE GAPS?

YOU ARE THE DIFFERENCE MAKER

As the difference maker in your own Life Story Timeline, how do your values withstand the tests that come your way? Do you acquiesce easily when pressured? Or do you stay true to yourself and what you believe is right and true?

We wouldn't have much regard for a hero in any story that gives up too soon in the plot.

What we expect is that our leaders never give up even if they are frequently prone to temptation. The human foibles and weaknesses keep us interested. We are eager to discover how the characters handle the challenges and will oftentimes root for the underdog if they demonstrate sufficient courage. We expect the hero will struggle. Otherwise there would be no story but merely a bland acting out of ordinary daily routines. The more difficult the challenge the better. It will keep us glued to our seats. It will be a book we can't put down or a movie we will watch again and again for its excitement, energy and empowering messages.

Does your Life Story Timeline empower others with its lessons learned, risks undertaken and opportunities seized?

As the leader of your Life Story Timeline what does your character communicate to the world?

Say the following phrases aloud while standing in front of a mirror. What does the person looking back at you communicate? Do you recognize confidence or fear? Does the person come across as self-assured or timid and uncertain? Practice until you get the result you want.

What does it mean when you can say to yourself?

I am a person of power.

I am committed.

I am responsible.

I persevere.

I am courageous.

I am tenacious.

I am honest.

I am trustworthy.

I respect others.

Take up your notebook once again. You are now ready to reflect upon what kind of leader you aspire to be. Or, if you do consider yourself to be a leader in life, then this is a time to consider an opportunity to recreate yourself.

Write a story with you as the hero. What is the situation? What challenge does the hero face in the story? How do they deal with the dilemma? What makes the hero take action and what action does the person take to help ensure as successful a positive outcome as possible?

Do you recognize yourself in this story? How close are you to realizing the vision of leadership you have for yourself? What people, places, events and things will help you to close some of the gaps or fill in the missing pieces? Consider your lifeline. Now incorporate the new information onto your map.

Now you are actively involved, with intention and strong resolve to create your future and, if necessary, to recreate yourself to fit a new reality that you now desire.

THOUGHT PROVOKING
QUOTES

Leadership is timeless.

Leadership takes time.

Leadership is a process, a path, a journey and
most important of all, a choice.

You choose leadership; leadership doesn't choose you.

Leadership is open to everyone, at every level
and has no limits as to who is a leader.

Leadership is a solitary path yet it involves having an impact on others.

Leaders reflect on their contribution, impact and legacy.

Leaders make mistakes; they know that is the way to learn.

Leaders grow, share and care.

- Jo Singel

A leader can observe from many different angles.

What looks the same to most people offers
numerous possibilities to the leader.

A leader is a hunter and planner knowing there are times when
the pursuit of the goal requires focus and perseverance.

- Jo Singel

It's always about the subtle contrasts. Some perspectives or views have more light than others.

Leaders seek the bright spots, however dim on the horizon they may be. They will sit and wait out the storm, knowing that they always pass even when they may leave destruction in their path.

Leaders pick themselves up and get to work on the plan to shed light on the dark areas and look for opportunities even when the prospects appear to be dim and remote.

Leaders keep the light in themselves knowing that life can interrupt any view: sunny, bright or dark.

- Jo Singel

Leaders decide which paths are worth pursuing. Some paths are more open than others. Does that mean those with fences around them shouldn't be pursued? Are they worth the climb? All paths have uncertain futures. Which ones to take and when are always questions for the leader.

- Jo Singel

Sometimes people live in environments and circumstances that are difficult to overcome with pithy platitudes and positive thinking language.

What helps those individuals aspire to be in leadership in life and in their communities? How deep is the pain that prevents the individual from climbing beyond where they are to where they could be?

There are no easy answers. No one said that leadership was easy.

- Jo Singel

Things get old and they decay. That is the cycle of life and death.

Unavoidable. Yet, while we are here there are so many things we can do to recreate and revitalize what's important…

Things change. Always. Sometimes for the better; sometimes for the worse.

But change they will. Who we "be" when things change will make all the difference in what we "do" and what we create as a result.

- Jo Singel

Sometimes you just have to hit the pause button and take a hard look at yourself. We can take ourselves a little too seriously sometimes. There are days when I wish I were a shadow lightly touching what is around me. That way I wouldn't make any mistakes. And then I remind myself of who I am and why I'm here.

- Jo Singel

Sometimes I feel alone on this path of forging a leadership identity. But then I look at the birds and their activity on the beach. They walk alone but nearly always touch base with their flock.

- Jo Singel

Leaders are almost always bridge builders.

They notice what's missing and find ways to solve problems.

Leaders can be very practical.

Yet they always have a "big picture" in mind.

The Verrazano Bridge in New York City was a vision that was beautifully realized.

Leaders take the long view but also see the details.

    - Jo Singel

Achieving satisfaction from completed goals gains you a new perspective from which to continue to set and achieve progressively challenging and bigger goals.

What is important now?

- Jo Singel

LEADERSHIP STORIES

LEARNING FROM OTHER'S WISDOM

Without a clear concept of your own history you will only be adding to more of what you already have. And that may not be nearly enough to get you to a place where you want and need to be in order to live a meaningful and purposeful life.

There may be something aching within you that wants to be expressed. You're not certain what it is and no one can tell you. You will need to discover this on your own.

Everything and everyone else is merely the "material" which can support you in your quest. Conversations, books and retreats will only get you so far.

It's important to remember that nothing stays exactly the same.

Either you are in charge of the change or you are at the effect of it.

Remaining in a position of "status quo" or stationary will only set you up to be a "sitting duck".

Regardless, no matter where you are or think you are right now, the path of leadership is a never-ending process of learning and growing.

Leadership is active involvement and engagement with life.

As already stated, getting there is not without its demands and costs in terms of time, energy and resources.

It may even cost you financially. You may choose a less lucrative path over one that could give you a greater monetary and ego-feeding payback.

Once again, only you can be the decider. No one else can do this important work of assessment but you.

A CEO

Consider a case where the CEO of a Fortune 200 company has oversight for the lives of thousands if not hundreds of thousands of people in a country other than his own. This is a true situation. The company lost a key military defense contract. Thousands of people were employed in a plant far from the continent where this CEO managed the organization. There was a great deal of pressure from the management team and the Board of Directors to close the plant where these people worked. There would be no work for a very long time. There was no contract that would provide a very large number of people with earning a viable living.

The CEO had to make the final decision. He was very distressed and torn about whether or not to close the plant. But he had to do it. Otherwise, the entire company including its fortunes and future would be at stake.

The plant closed and four thousand people were displaced.

The CEO openly wept over the decision. But it had to be done. He was in a business where he was responsible for the entire organization. Even though he regarded the business as a family institution, he was answerable to the Board of Directors, the Wall Street analysts and the shareholders of the company.

The CEO took responsibility for the overall health and welfare of the organization regardless of his personal feelings for the individuals involved.

If you were the CEO what would you or could you have done differently, if anything?

Do you believe he was justified in his actions or might there have been other alternatives?

If you were his second in command what questions might you have asked or approaches taken?

What would you do if you were the individual in this leadership role in a similar situation where people's livelihoods were at stake?

A STORY ABOUT MARY

Mary, a corporate professional decides to take stock of her life and complete a lifeline.

What she discovers is that when certain people were in her life she felt more content and fulfilled in what she was doing. For Mary, strong and caring relationships coincided with success in her job. Conversely, when Mary was feeling alone and alienated from family and friends, her career took a downhill slide and she found herself in a situation where she felt she had to start over again. After Mary completed her lifeline she concluded that her value for nurturing and authentic relationships were a top priority. In the future, she would ensure that no matter how hectic her career became she would plan time to attend family gatherings, have dinner with good friends and not lose touch as she pursued her professional goals.

This is the value of taking time to examine and assess people, places and events taking place over the course of time and significance they may have held.

Perhaps you met an individual who became a mentor and you discovered things about yourself that you would not have otherwise noticed.

This may be an indication that at certain times you need to cultivate certain types of relationships and place yourself into situations that are unfamiliar and even uncomfortable.

It is easy to slide into the drift of life and not notice that you are far from where you wanted to be.

Sometimes an unfamiliar place can act as a challenge for you to explore different aspects of your talents and aspirations.

You may also discover that a retreat or workshop you took had a powerful effect and that you recreated yourself as a result.

Whether it be a person, a place, an event or a thing it's important to understand your own particular motivators and how to seek them out, nurture them and incorporate them into your life.

A STORY ABOUT MARK

Consider the story of Mark who, as a young man grew up in a small steel mill town in a mountainous and isolated area of Pennsylvania far away from any large city. The chief source of entertainment was high school football games, movies in the one cinema on Main Street and for the elders, the local tap room where stories and punches were frequently exchanged especially around the time the weekly paycheck was cashed.

For the most part, people in the town were poor. The town had a right and wrong side of the tracks where the better off could compare themselves to those who had less than they did. The houses were square wooden boxes placed closely together on levels that went higher and higher up the mountain upon which the town was built. Because of the day and night operation of the steel mill, there was a persistent red dust that covered every car, fence and house within a ten mile radius. People mingled on Main Street where food, clothing and the occasional trinkets were purchased. Despite the poverty, life was stable, families were strong and for the most part no one starved to death. Beggars on the streets were simply non-existent.

His mother and father decided, as good parents will do, to relocate the family in order to achieve a higher standard of living. Mark's father worked hard to educate himself. He raised himself up from steel-mill worker to head of a music department in a school in a middle-class neighborhood miles from his hometown. Mark could have easily followed in his father's footsteps. Himself a gifted musician, he could have continued as a respectable citizen in the town where his family was known and he had built strong ties and good friendships. But as the years passed, Mark began to formulate a dream of his own. Always a strong and independent child who took his life in his own hands, upon graduation he joined the Air Force, left home and never returned except to visit. Mark's experience of life was far different from his parents. While in the Air Force, his exposure to different people and new ideas motivated him to dream a bigger dream - to live and work in New York City.

Mark was an intelligent young man with strong interpersonal skills. At an early age he was personable, charismatic, persuasive, kind and caring. He made friends easily and people wanted to know him wherever he went. He worked hard at his job, took responsibility for whatever task he embarked upon and before long he was living and working in Manhattan, managing people in a respectable corporate position.

Why is Mark's story in a book about leadership? The meaning of Mark's story is that, from the time he was a young boy and growing into young manhood, Mark had a strong sense of self. Was he always on track with his goals? No. Did he always do the right and correct thing? No. But what he did was to continue to follow his heart, questioning the "rightness" of the situation he was in and whether or not it served him and others in positive ways.

Today, Mark is a husband, father, grandfather and retired from a position where his job was to help others learn, grow and develop themselves into their best selves regardless of their beginnings, resources and/or current skills. He did his work with passion and the assuredness of someone who has empathy for others' circumstances, their capacity to learn and their willingness to do the work.

Mark is a leader of his life. He is a mentor, coach, and role model for others who strive to create their own path in life, relying upon themselves as their own best teachers and forging a leadership identity that is unique, powerful and impactful. Mark carries himself in a way that others think he is man who is a wealthy individual who occupies a powerful position in the world of business. Mark is unique. He has never been wealthy nor does he occupy a position of great power and authority. But within himself he is both.

A STORY ABOUT JOHN

John came to America at the age of eleven months. His mother, father and siblings had already made the journey not because they wanted to leave their homeland but because they were unable to feed themselves. From the news carried by friends and relatives, they headed for America as their only hope for survival.

Several years after their arrival in their new country, the family hit another period of scarcity and it was decided that the mother and her children should return to their homeland and seek help there. The mother was pregnant with her fourth and last child.

As a result, John was born in a small town outside of Naples, Italy. This fact would haunt him for half of his lifetime. John was never comfortable with his heritage. Growing up in an Italian-American ghetto with barely enough food to eat or clothing to wear to school, he had a self-consciousness about him that his siblings did not possess. He got into trouble along the way but was never imprisoned.

At the age of eighteen he joined the Army and was immediately drafted into World War II. The only problem was that, still denying his birthplace, he lied on his application that he was born in America. Fortunately for him, the Army was looking for any able bodied man to fight in the war. John was naturalized and shipped overseas for three hard years of heavy fighting. He returned to America at the end of the war injured, with his purple heart and other medals in hand. He married the woman he left three years ago and began his career as a Laborer in the U.S. Government.

Never having graduated from High School, John made his way up through the ranks and joined the Department of the Navy as a Firefighter for their naval ammunition bases. A few years later he became Chief and from there on he held positions of leadership and authority. In the evenings John studied hard to learn the fundamentals of engineering and chemistry. He taught many individuals with much higher levels of education. The only reason he retired was a severe back problem that kept him hunched over in pain for the remainder of his life.

When John passed away in his early sixties, he left a legacy of respect, power, self-confidence, presence, discipline, accomplishment and a family who honored him. No one would ever doubt this man's commitment and dedication. He was honest, hard-working and had a high regard for any individual he met. John was a self-created man.

LEADERS END WITH A CALL TO ACTION

WHAT DO YOU WANT TO LEARN...IN ORDER TO MAKE A POSITIVE DIFFERENCE AS A VISIBLE AND DELIBERATE CREATOR OF RAPID CHANGE?

APPLY WHAT YOU LEARNED AS A VISIBLE AND DELIBERATE CREATOR OF RAPID CHANGE WITH A WELL-DEFINED SOCIAL IMPACT INITIATIVE

Enroll other Deliberate Creators to join you in making rapid change in a social impact initiative (or corporate social responsibility goal) that needs to be urgently addressed.

1. Form a Team
   a. Consider who should be on the team and what their roles will be

2. Conduct a Team Meeting
   a. Set Ground Rules
      Set Team Goals
      i. Individual activities
      ii. Responsibilities
      iii. Timeline
      iv. Accountabilities
      v. Metrics

3. Enroll Mentors for Deliberate Creators

4. Create success metrics for: Social Impact Initiative, Team and Individuals

5. Find others who have worked on similar initiatives.
   a. Conduct Peer to Peer Knowledge Sharing: Who has done what you are setting out to do and what can you learn from them?
   b. Learn from their successes and failures

6. Identify additional resources such as Influencers and Subject Matter Experts who can enhance, broaden and stretch what you already know and what you need to learn

7. Conduct After Learning reviews as the initiative progresses

8. Conduct individual and team feedback sessions

9. Create time and space for individual action planning and personal development goal setting

10. Create a Life Story Timeline for the Initiative

IMPORTANT CONSIDERATIONS FOR SOCIAL IMPACT INITIATIVES

- **WHAT IS THE PROBLEM TO BE SOLVED?**
- **WHAT IS THE DISRUPTIVE IDEA OR INNOVATION?**
- **WHO BENEFITS FROM THE POSSIBLE SOLUTION?**
- **WHAT ARE THE SOCIAL IMPACT INTENDED RESULTS?**
- **WHAT MEASURES WILL BE USEFUL ACROSS THE LIFETIME OF THE SOLUTION?**
  - **IS THE SOLUTION SUSTAINABLE?**
  - **IS IT REPLICABLE?**
  - **CAN OTHERS LEARN FROM IT?**

MY GRATITUDE TO MENTORS, TEACHERS AND
INDIVIDUALS WHOSE ABUNDANT GUIDANCE,
INSPIRATION, LOVE AND INFLUENCE HAVE
AND CONTINUE TO HAVE A POSITIVE
IMPACT ON MY LIFE AND WORK.

My Father, Carmen Pagano

My Husband, Don Singel

My Son, Jonathan Singel

Marta Antonelli

Veta Bates

Dr. John Bell

Josephine Bonavitacola

Larry Condon

Patrice Hall

Frank Hickey

Dr. Stephen John

Sister Helena Mary, I.H.M.

Stephen McCarthy

LuEsther Mertz

Joan Rose

I dedicate this book to Madeleine Jo Singel, my grand-daughter, in the hopes it will serve as a guide and legacy of the practice, study and understanding of leadership and that the main values will withstand the test of time and remain viable in the future.

www.ingramcontent.com/pod-product-compliance
Lightning Source LLC
Chambersburg PA
CBHW021357210526
45463CB00001B/131